INTRODUCTION TO CLOUD COMPUTING KEY CONCEPTS AND MODELS

Overview of cloud computing, service models (IaaS, PaaS, SaaS), and deployment models (public, private, hybrid)

NATHAN WESTWOOD

TABLE OF CONTENTS

ABOUT THE AUTHOR!

Dr. Nathan Westwood

Biography:

Dr. Nathan Westwood is a pioneering technologist known for his exceptional contributions to the fields of software development, cloud computing, and artificial intelligence. With a passion for innovation and a relentless drive to solve complex problems, Nathan has become a prominent figure in the tech industry, shaping the future of digital technology.

Born and raised in Silicon Valley, Nathan's interest in technology started at a young age. His fascination with computers and coding led him to pursue a degree in Computer Science from Stanford University, where he excelled academically and honed his skills in programming and software engineering. During his time at Stanford, Nathan was involved in several cutting-edge projects that sparked his interest in AI and cloud technologies.

After graduating, Nathan joined a leading tech firm where he played a key role in developing cloud-based solutions that revolutionized data storage and analytics. His work in the early stages of cloud computing set the foundation for modern infrastructure-as-a-service (IaaS) platforms, earning him recognition as one of the industry's emerging stars. As a lead engineer, Nathan was instrumental in launching products that have since become industry standards.

Nathan's entrepreneurial spirit led him to co-found his own tech startup focused on AI-driven automation tools for businesses. Under his leadership, the company rapidly gained traction, attracting both investors and clients who were eager to leverage his innovative AI solutions to streamline operations and improve efficiency. Nathan's commitment to pushing the boundaries of what's possible in tech quickly earned him a reputation as a visionary leader.

Known for his expertise in machine learning, Nathan has also worked with several large tech companies, advising on the integration of AI and data science into their operations. His work has spanned various sectors, including healthcare, finance, and manufacturing, where he has helped organizations harness the power of data and automation to achieve exponential growth.

Beyond his technical achievements, Nathan is a sought-after speaker at global tech conferences, where he shares his insights on the future of cloud computing, artificial intelligence, and the ethical challenges posed by emerging technologies. His thought leadership and commitment to ethical innovation have made him a respected voice in the tech community.

In addition to his professional accomplishments, Nathan is deeply passionate about mentoring the next generation of tech leaders. He regularly contributes to educational programs and initiatives designed to inspire young minds and equip them with the skills necessary to thrive in the ever-evolving tech landscape.

Nathan Westwood continues to be a trailblazer in the tech industry, shaping the future of technology with his innovative ideas, entrepreneurial spirit, and commitment to making a positive impact on the world.

CHAPTER 1: WHAT IS CLOUD COMPUTING?

Introduction to Cloud Computing

Cloud computing is one of the most transformative technologies of the 21st century, and its influence spans across various industries. At its core, cloud computing refers to the delivery of computing services—such as storage, processing power, and software—over the internet (the "cloud") rather than using local servers or personal devices.

In the traditional model of computing, individuals and businesses had to manage and maintain their own infrastructure, whether it was for data storage, computing power, or running software. This required not only significant capital investment in hardware but also ongoing maintenance costs for ensuring that everything ran smoothly.

Cloud computing turns this model on its head. Instead of owning and maintaining expensive infrastructure, organizations can rent access to computing resources through cloud service providers (CSPs) such as Amazon Web Services (AWS), Microsoft Azure, or Google Cloud. This shift allows businesses to focus on what they do best—delivering value to customers—without worrying about maintaining infrastructure.

Key Elements of Cloud Computing

- **On-Demand Self-Service**: With cloud computing, users can provision resources like storage and computing power without needing direct interaction with the service provider. This self-service model eliminates bottlenecks and streamlines the provisioning of resources.

- **Broad Network Access**: Cloud services are accessible via the internet, which means users can access their resources from anywhere at any time, as long as they have a connection.

- **Resource Pooling**: Cloud providers pool resources to serve multiple customers, using multi-tenant models. This means that the computing power, storage, and networks are dynamically allocated and reassigned based on customer demand.

- **Rapid Elasticity**: Cloud computing resources can be scaled up or down quickly and efficiently, based on the demand, providing flexibility and ensuring that users are not paying for resources they don't need.

- **Measured Service**: Cloud computing follows a pay-as-you-go model where users only pay for the services they consume, making it an attractive option for businesses of all sizes.

How Cloud Computing Transformed Technology

Before the rise of cloud computing, scaling an application required businesses to invest in physical servers, often overprovisioning to account for unpredictable traffic spikes. This meant companies had to spend heavily on infrastructure that would remain idle for most of the time. Cloud computing, on the other hand, enables businesses to scale their infrastructure dynamically, ensuring that resources are allocated based on demand.

Moreover, cloud computing has democratized technology, allowing startups and small businesses to access resources previously only available to large enterprises. By removing the need for heavy upfront investments, cloud services have lowered the barrier to entry for companies across various sectors.

Why Cloud Computing?

The benefits of cloud computing extend far beyond just cost savings. Cloud computing has driven digital transformation in numerous sectors, enabling innovation, improving operational efficiency, and enabling companies to scale more rapidly.

1. Healthcare

In healthcare, cloud computing has played a pivotal role in the modernization of IT systems. Hospitals and healthcare providers now leverage cloud services to store electronic health records (EHRs), manage patient data, and support telemedicine initiatives. The ability to access critical patient information from any device connected to the internet has improved the efficiency of care and enhanced the patient experience.

Cloud computing has also made it possible for healthcare providers to analyze vast amounts of data in real time, improving decision-making processes. For instance, machine learning models can be deployed in the cloud to predict patient outcomes or assist with diagnosing diseases, enabling doctors to make more informed decisions.

Example: Imagine a hospital utilizing a cloud-based platform like AWS for managing patient records. Physicians and nurses can securely access up-to-date records from anywhere, improving care coordination.

2. Manufacturing

In manufacturing, cloud computing has optimized supply chains, enhanced the performance of factory operations, and streamlined the management of production processes. Through the Internet of Things (IoT) connected to cloud platforms, machines in manufacturing plants can continuously monitor their performance, share data, and predict maintenance needs.

Additionally, the cloud allows manufacturers to analyze production data and improve operational efficiency in real time. This data-driven approach helps to reduce costs, prevent downtime, and ensure that supply chains are responsive to changes in demand.

Example: A company like General Electric (GE) uses cloud-based applications to monitor industrial equipment, providing real-time data to optimize production and maintenance schedules.

3. Education

Cloud computing has transformed the education sector by enabling institutions to host virtual classrooms, store large volumes of educational materials, and offer e-learning platforms. This is particularly useful in providing access to quality education in remote or underserved regions, where local infrastructure might not support traditional classroom-based learning.

Cloud services have also improved collaboration, with tools like Google Docs, Microsoft Teams, and Zoom allowing students and educators to collaborate, share documents, and engage in online classes seamlessly.

Example: A university might leverage AWS or Google Cloud to host an e-learning platform, enabling students to access lecture content, participate in discussions, and complete assignments remotely.

4. Retail

Retail businesses have benefitted greatly from cloud computing by moving inventory management, sales transactions, and customer data into the cloud. Cloud computing allows retailers to provide omnichannel shopping experiences, where customers can shop both online and in physical stores, with seamless integration between the two.

Additionally, cloud-based analytics tools enable retailers to analyze consumer behavior and tailor their offerings in real-time, leading to a more personalized customer experience and better-targeted marketing campaigns.

Example: An e-commerce store might use cloud computing to handle everything from customer orders to inventory management. With cloud-based services, they can quickly scale to accommodate traffic surges during peak shopping seasons like Black Friday.

Cloud vs. Traditional IT Infrastructure

Traditional IT Infrastructure

In the traditional IT infrastructure model, companies purchase, set up, and maintain physical servers on-site. They are responsible for the upkeep of the hardware, the management of data, and the security of their IT systems. This requires significant capital investment and ongoing operational costs for power, cooling, and maintenance.

While this model offers control over every aspect of the infrastructure, it's often expensive and time-consuming. The physical hardware quickly becomes outdated, and scaling operations typically requires purchasing additional equipment, which again incurs additional costs.

Cloud Computing as a Utility

A more modern analogy would be to think of cloud computing as a utility service, such as electricity or water. Just like we don't need to own and maintain power plants to access electricity, we don't need to own or maintain servers to use cloud computing. Instead of worrying about the infrastructure, cloud users can simply "plug in" to the service and use what they need.

In the case of cloud computing, the provider (such as AWS or Azure) owns and maintains the infrastructure, and customers can scale their usage as needed. If you need more computing power or storage, you can request it through a simple interface. You only pay for the resources you use, much like how you're billed based on the amount of electricity you consume each month.

Key Comparison:

Feature	Traditional IT Infrastructure	Cloud Computing
Cost	High upfront and maintenance costs	Pay-as-you-go model, flexible
Scaling	Manual scaling, additional purchases	Automatically scales with demand
Control	Full control over the system	Limited control over the infrastructure, but more flexibility
Maintenance	Time-consuming and costly	Managed by the service provider

Why Cloud is a Game-Changer

Cloud computing eliminates the need for businesses to manage and maintain complex IT systems. It reduces upfront capital investment, simplifies scaling, and lowers the burden of ongoing maintenance. Moreover, with services like IaaS, PaaS, and SaaS, businesses can focus more on delivering value and less on managing infrastructure.

Practical Project

Step 1: Choosing Your Cloud Provider

To start, we'll create a free-tier account with one of the leading cloud providers. Let's look at the steps involved with AWS, Google Cloud, and Microsoft Azure. All three offer free-tier services that allow you to get hands-on experience with cloud infrastructure, even if you're just starting out.

- **AWS**: AWS provides 12 months of free-tier services, including EC2 instances and S3 storage.

- **Google Cloud**: Google Cloud offers $300 in credits to use over the first 90 days.

- **Azure**: Azure offers a free account with $200 in credits for the first 30 days and access to free services for 12 months.

Step 2: Signing Up for a Free Account

- **AWS**: Go to the AWS Free Tier page and click "Create a Free Account". Follow the on-screen instructions to enter your information, including billing details. Don't worry, AWS won't charge you unless you exceed the free tier usage.

- **Google Cloud**: Head to the Google Cloud Free page. Sign up and claim your free credits. You'll also need to enter billing details, but you won't be charged unless you exceed the free usage limits.

- **Azure**: Visit the Azure Free page and create a free account. You'll receive $200 in credits and access to a range of free services for 12 months.

Step 3: Creating Your First Virtual Machine

Now that you have your free-tier account set up, let's create your first virtual machine (VM).

- **AWS**:

    1. Navigate to the EC2 Dashboard in the AWS Management Console.

    2. Select "Launch Instance" to start a new VM.

    3. Choose an Amazon Machine Image (AMI)—for example, the free Ubuntu Linux AMI.

    4. Select the instance type (t2.micro for the free tier).

    5. Follow the prompts to configure the instance (e.g., add security groups, set up key pairs).

    6. Launch the instance and connect via SSH.

- **Google Cloud**:

    1. Go to the Google Cloud Console and navigate to the VM instances page.

    2. Click "Create Instance" and choose the machine type (e2-micro for the free tier).

3. Set your region and zone, and choose your operating system (e.g., Ubuntu).

4. Create and configure firewall rules for SSH access.

5. Click "Create" and connect to your VM using SSH.

- **Azure:**

    1. Go to the Azure portal and navigate to the "Virtual Machines" section.

    2. Click "Add" to create a new VM.

    3. Choose the operating system (Windows or Linux) and size (B1S for the free tier).

    4. Set up the network, security settings, and SSH keys.

    5. Click "Review + Create" and connect to your VM.

Conclusion

Cloud computing is revolutionizing how we interact with technology. From increasing accessibility and lowering costs to enabling rapid innovation, the cloud offers immense potential. This chapter has provided a foundational understanding of cloud computing and its applications, while the practical project has given you your first hands-on experience with cloud infrastructure.

CHAPTER 2:
EXPLORING CLOUD SERVICE MODELS: IAAS, PAAS, AND SAAS

Introduction to Service Models

Cloud computing is revolutionizing the way businesses manage their infrastructure, develop applications, and deploy software solutions. The evolution of cloud computing has introduced different service models to meet the diverse needs of businesses, developers, and end-users. These models are typically broken down into three core categories: **Infrastructure as a Service (IaaS), Platform as a Service (PaaS)**, and **Software as a Service (SaaS)**.

Each of these models offers distinct advantages and is suited for different types of users and use cases. Understanding the nuances between them will help you decide which service is right for you, whether you're a developer building the next big app or a business looking to streamline your IT infrastructure.

IaaS (Infrastructure as a Service)

Infrastructure as a Service (IaaS) provides the foundational building blocks for IT infrastructure in the cloud. IaaS allows you to rent virtualized computing resources over the internet, including virtual machines, storage, and networking. Essentially, it provides the hardware components of an IT infrastructure, but without the physical limitations. Instead of owning and maintaining servers, IaaS users can access computing resources through cloud providers such as **AWS** (Amazon Web Services), **Google Cloud**, and **Microsoft Azure**.

IaaS Overview

IaaS is best suited for users who need flexibility and control over their virtualized computing environment. Unlike PaaS, which abstracts the infrastructure for you, IaaS gives you direct access to virtual machines (VMs) and networking, making it ideal for developers, system administrators, and companies with specific needs around server configuration and control.

IaaS providers typically offer a broad range of virtualized services, including:

- **Compute Resources**: Virtual machines (VMs) that run applications and workloads.

- **Storage**: Scalable storage solutions, such as object storage (e.g., Amazon S3), file storage, and block storage.

- **Networking**: Virtual networks, load balancers, VPNs, and firewalls to ensure your infrastructure is secure and well-managed.

- **Backup and Disaster Recovery**: Services designed to ensure your data is protected, even in the case of failure.

EXAMPLES OF IaaS PROVIDERS

- **Amazon Web Services (AWS)**: AWS is the leader in the IaaS market, offering services like **Amazon EC2** (Elastic Compute Cloud) for running virtual machines and **Amazon S3** for scalable storage.

- **Google Cloud Platform (GCP)**: Google offers services like **Google Compute Engine** (GCE) for creating virtual machines, **Google Cloud Storage**, and **Google Virtual Private Cloud** (VPC) for networking.

- **Microsoft Azure**: Microsoft's Azure platform provides compute services through **Azure Virtual Machines**, **Blob Storage** for scalable data storage, and **Azure Networking** for secure communication between virtualized resources.

Why Use IaaS?

IaaS offers flexibility and control over infrastructure, without the need for expensive hardware investments. It's cost-effective because you only pay for the resources you use (pay-as-you-go model), and you can scale your resources up or down depending on your needs. Businesses can avoid the complexity of managing physical infrastructure while still retaining control over their operating systems, applications, and data.

Practical Project: Launching Your First Virtual Machine

Now, let's walk through the process of launching your first virtual machine (VM) using AWS EC2. You'll learn how to set up an instance, configure networking, and connect to it via SSH. This will give you hands-on experience with IaaS and its core services.

Steps to launch a Virtual Machine using AWS EC2:

1. **Sign Up for AWS**: Create a free-tier AWS account if you haven't already. AWS provides 750 hours per month of free EC2 usage for the first 12 months.

2. **Launch EC2 Instance**: Navigate to the **EC2 Dashboard** in the AWS Management Console and click on "Launch

Instance." Choose a free-tier eligible instance type (e.g., **t2.micro**).

3. **Choose an AMI**: Select an Amazon Machine Image (AMI). For simplicity, we'll use **Ubuntu Server 20.04** as an example.

4. **Configure Instance**: Choose the default settings for networking, and configure any additional settings such as **key pairs** for SSH access.

5. **Set Up Security Groups**: Add rules to allow SSH access (port 22) from your IP address.

6. **Launch and Connect**: After the instance is launched, select the instance and note the **Public IP**. Connect to the instance via SSH using the following command:

bash

```
ssh -i /path/to/your-key.pem ubuntu@<Public-IP>
```

Once you're connected, you can start installing software and configuring your server.

PaaS (Platform as a Service)

Platform as a Service (PaaS) is a cloud service model that provides a platform and environment for developing, testing, and deploying applications. Unlike IaaS, which gives you the virtualized infrastructure, PaaS abstracts much of the infrastructure management, allowing developers to focus on writing code rather than worrying about servers, storage, and networking.

PaaS Overview

PaaS provides an integrated development environment (IDE) with all the tools, libraries, and frameworks you need to build applications. It typically includes everything from application hosting to databases, caching, and logging services. PaaS platforms allow developers to upload their code and have the platform handle all the backend infrastructure, including scaling, security, and maintenance.

Examples of PaaS Providers

- **Heroku**: One of the most popular PaaS platforms for developers. It supports multiple programming languages such as Ruby, Java, Node.js, Python, and PHP.

- **Google App Engine**: Google's managed platform for building and deploying web applications and APIs. It supports Java, Python, PHP, Go, and other languages.

- **Microsoft Azure App Service**: Azure's platform for building and deploying web apps, APIs, and mobile backends. It supports a wide range of programming languages and frameworks.

Why Use PaaS?

PaaS is ideal for developers who want to build and deploy applications quickly, without worrying about the underlying infrastructure. It handles scaling, patching, and load balancing automatically, which allows developers to focus on what matters most—the code.

Practical Project: Deploying a Simple App on Heroku

Let's walk through deploying a simple web app on **Heroku**. You'll be deploying a basic **Node.js** app with a MongoDB database.

Steps to deploy on Heroku:

1. **Sign Up for Heroku**: Create a free Heroku account at heroku.com.

2. **Install Heroku CLI**: Install the Heroku Command Line Interface (CLI) on your machine.

3. **Create a Node.js App**: Create a simple Node.js app using Express.js. Here's a basic example:

javascript

```javascript
const express = require('express');
const app = express();
app.get('/', (req, res) => res.send('Hello, World!'));
app.listen(process.env.PORT || 5000);
```

4. **Initialize Git Repository**: In your app's folder, initialize a Git repository:

bash

```bash
git init
```

5. **Deploy to Heroku**: Log in to Heroku via the CLI, create a new app, and deploy:

bash

```bash
heroku login
```

```
heroku create my-app-name
git push heroku master
```

Your app will now be live, and you can visit it by navigating to https://my-app-name.herokuapp.com.

SaaS (Software as a Service): Accessing Software Over the Cloud

Software as a Service (SaaS) is the cloud service model most familiar to everyday users. SaaS allows individuals and businesses to access software applications over the internet without the need for installation, maintenance, or upgrades.

In this model, software is hosted and maintained by a service provider, and users access it via a web browser or app. SaaS has become ubiquitous in both business and personal use, offering everything from email and productivity tools to project management and customer relationship management (CRM) software.

SaaS Overview

SaaS provides a complete software solution. For businesses, it eliminates the need for internal software management, and for users, it means instant access to the tools they need, without the hassle of installation and upgrades.

Examples of SaaS Providers

- **Google Workspace**: A suite of productivity tools, including Gmail, Google Docs, Google Drive, and Google Meet. These applications are accessed via a web browser and allow for seamless collaboration.

- **Microsoft Office 365**: A cloud-based version of Microsoft Office, including Word, Excel, PowerPoint, Outlook, and more, with the added benefits of cloud storage and collaboration.

- **Salesforce**: A leading CRM platform that helps businesses manage their customer relationships, track sales, and integrate various business functions.

Why Use SaaS?

SaaS is ideal for businesses that need ready-made applications without the overhead of infrastructure management. SaaS solutions are typically subscription-based, and the software provider handles updates, security, and scalability.

Practical Project: Using Microsoft Office 365

Let's walk through how to access and use Microsoft Office 365. This SaaS platform provides an excellent way for businesses and individuals to manage documents, emails, and spreadsheets, all in the cloud.

Steps to get started with Office 365:

1. **Sign Up for Office 365**: Go to the Office 365 website and sign up for a free trial or subscription.

2. **Access Tools**: Once signed in, you can access tools like Word, Excel, and PowerPoint directly from your browser or desktop app.

3. **Collaborate**: Share documents and collaborate with others in real-time using OneDrive or SharePoint.

Practical Project: Choose One of the Service Models (IaaS, PaaS, or SaaS) and Set Up a Service Using the Platform of Your Choice

Now that you've learned the differences between IaaS, PaaS, and SaaS, it's time to choose one model and implement it. Whether you choose to set up a virtual machine in IaaS, deploy a web app in PaaS, or start using a SaaS tool like Office 365 or Google Workspace, the goal is to gain hands-on experience with cloud service models and see how they fit your needs.

Conclusion

Cloud computing's service models—**IaaS**, **PaaS**, and **SaaS**—offer distinct solutions to meet the varying needs of businesses and developers. Understanding these models allows you to make informed decisions based on your specific use case, whether that's managing virtual infrastructure, building applications, or leveraging powerful software tools. The hands-on projects provided in this chapter give you the foundation to explore these service models in more depth, and the knowledge you gain will empower you to start building solutions in the cloud.

CHAPTER 3: UNDERSTANDING CLOUD DEPLOYMENT MODELS

Overview of Cloud Deployment Models

In the world of cloud computing, the way services and infrastructure are deployed plays a significant role in defining how resources are accessed, managed, and secured. The choice of cloud deployment model directly impacts how businesses scale, their cost structure, and the level of control they maintain over their infrastructure.

The primary cloud deployment models are:

- **Public Cloud**

- **Private Cloud**

- **Hybrid Cloud**

Each of these models has its own set of advantages and trade-offs, depending on the specific needs of the organization. These differences stem from the type of infrastructure used, the level of control over that infrastructure, and how resources are accessed and managed.

Public Cloud

The **public cloud** is the most widely adopted cloud deployment model, offering on-demand access to a wide variety of computing resources over the internet. Public cloud services are owned, operated, and maintained by third-party cloud service providers (CSPs) such as **Amazon Web Services (AWS)**, **Google Cloud Platform (GCP)**, and **Microsoft Azure**.

Key Characteristics of Public Cloud:

- **Resource Sharing**: The infrastructure and services in a public cloud are shared among multiple organizations or tenants. The cloud provider owns the physical hardware and software, and tenants access it over the internet.

- **Scalability and Flexibility**: Public clouds are known for their ability to scale quickly and efficiently. Users can add or remove resources such as computing power, storage, and networking capabilities based on their needs.

- **Cost-Efficiency**: The pay-as-you-go model allows businesses to only pay for what they use. This eliminates the need for upfront capital investment in physical hardware and reduces long-term maintenance costs.

- **Multi-Tenant Architecture**: Since the cloud infrastructure is shared, each tenant operates in an isolated virtual environment, ensuring that data and workloads remain secure from other users.

Use Cases for Public Cloud:

1. **Web Hosting and E-Commerce**: Public clouds are ideal for hosting websites and e-commerce platforms that need to scale rapidly based on demand. For instance, AWS's **Elastic Compute Cloud (EC2)** allows businesses to dynamically scale up or down based on traffic fluctuations, which is perfect for handling spikes during promotions or sales events.

2. **Development and Testing**: Developers can take advantage of public clouds to create scalable and cost-efficient environments for application development and testing. By provisioning virtual machines and containers, they can replicate production environments and deploy new versions of applications in a matter of minutes.

3. **Big Data and Analytics**: Public clouds are a perfect fit for businesses that need to analyze large volumes of data. Services like Google Cloud's **BigQuery** or AWS's **Redshift** provide the scalability and computational power required to process and analyze vast datasets.

Examples of Public Cloud Providers:

- **AWS (Amazon Web Services)**: The leader in the public cloud space, AWS offers a wide range of services including computing, storage, networking, machine learning, and data analytics.

- **Google Cloud Platform (GCP)**: Known for its high-performance computing, GCP is favored for machine learning and data analytics with services like **BigQuery** and **TensorFlow**.

- **Microsoft Azure**: Offering a variety of cloud services for computing, analytics, storage, and networking, Azure is particularly popular with enterprises using Microsoft products like **Office 365** and **Active Directory**.

Advantages of Public Cloud:

- **Scalability**: The public cloud allows businesses to scale their resources up or down depending on usage without significant upfront investments.

- **Reduced Operational Complexity**: By offloading infrastructure management to cloud providers, organizations can focus on innovation rather than IT maintenance.

- **Global Reach**: Public cloud providers have data centers around the world, which ensures that businesses can deploy applications with low-latency access for users across multiple geographic locations.

Disadvantages of Public Cloud:

- **Limited Control**: Since the infrastructure is owned by third parties, users have less control over the configuration and security of the underlying hardware.

- **Security Concerns**: While public cloud providers offer robust security features, some businesses may find it challenging to meet compliance and security requirements when their data is stored off-premises.

Private Cloud: Total Control with Enhanced Security

The **private cloud** is a cloud environment that is used exclusively by one organization. It can be hosted on-premises within an organization's own data center or managed by a third-party provider, but it is not shared with other organizations. This model is preferred by organizations that require complete control over their infrastructure and need to comply with stringent regulatory or security requirements.

Key Characteristics of Private Cloud:

- **Exclusive Use**: Unlike public clouds, a private cloud is dedicated to a single organization, ensuring that all resources—compute, storage, and networking—are reserved exclusively for that entity.

- **Customization**: Private clouds can be customized to fit the specific needs of the organization, offering more granular control over security, configuration, and management.

- **Security and Compliance**: Since the infrastructure is dedicated to one organization, private clouds offer a higher level of security. This makes private clouds an ideal choice for organizations in regulated industries like healthcare, finance, or government.

Use Cases for Private Cloud:

1. **Healthcare Organizations**: Private clouds are ideal for healthcare organizations that need to comply with strict privacy regulations such as **HIPAA**. Private clouds allow

them to store sensitive patient data securely while maintaining full control over the infrastructure.

2. **Financial Institutions**: Banks and other financial institutions use private clouds to ensure data security and compliance with regulations like **PCI DSS**. A private cloud enables them to store and process financial data without exposing it to potential risks in a public environment.

3. **Government Agencies**: Government entities, which are often subject to stringent data sovereignty and security requirements, may prefer a private cloud to ensure complete control over the infrastructure and maintain compliance with legal requirements.

Examples of Private Cloud Providers:

- **VMware vSphere**: VMware's private cloud offering provides organizations with tools for creating and managing virtualized environments within their own data centers.

- **OpenStack**: OpenStack is an open-source platform for building and managing private clouds. It allows organizations to create a customized private cloud environment tailored to their needs.

- **Microsoft Azure Stack**: Azure Stack is a private cloud solution that brings the power of Azure services on-premises. It allows organizations to build their own private cloud while maintaining compatibility with Azure services.

Advantages of Private Cloud:

- **Control**: Organizations have full control over the hardware, software, and network configurations. This enables them to customize their infrastructure based on their specific needs.

- **Enhanced Security**: Since the cloud infrastructure is not shared with other organizations, private clouds offer more stringent security controls and better protection for sensitive data.

- **Compliance**: Private clouds help organizations meet regulatory and compliance requirements by offering the ability to store data on-premises or within a specific region.

Disadvantages of Private Cloud:

- **Higher Costs**: Building and maintaining a private cloud can be costly. It requires significant capital investment in hardware and software, as well as ongoing maintenance costs.

- **Scalability Limitations**: Unlike public clouds, which offer nearly limitless scalability, private clouds can be constrained by the physical hardware and resources owned by the organization.

Hybrid Cloud: Combining the Best of Both Worlds

The **hybrid cloud** model is a combination of public and private clouds, designed to offer organizations the flexibility of scaling resources on-demand while maintaining control over critical, sensitive data. This model enables businesses to leverage the strengths of both public and private clouds, providing a balance between control, cost efficiency, and scalability.

Key Characteristics of Hybrid Cloud:

- **Seamless Integration**: Hybrid cloud architectures enable organizations to integrate public and private cloud resources seamlessly, allowing workloads to be distributed between both environments.

- **Workload Mobility**: With a hybrid cloud model, organizations can move workloads between public and private clouds based on their needs. For example, they might keep sensitive data in the private cloud while scaling other workloads in the public cloud.

- **Flexibility**: The hybrid cloud model offers greater flexibility by allowing businesses to optimize their cloud environments for different workloads. For instance, non-sensitive applications can run in the public cloud, while mission-critical applications can be hosted in a private cloud.

Use Cases for Hybrid Cloud:

1. **E-Commerce Platforms**: An e-commerce platform might use a hybrid cloud model to run its customer-facing website on the public cloud, while keeping sensitive customer data (e.g., credit card information) in a private cloud for added security.

2. **Disaster Recovery**: Many organizations use hybrid clouds for disaster recovery solutions. By backing up data and

running failover services in the public cloud, businesses ensure continuity even if their private cloud infrastructure experiences issues.

3. **Data Sovereignty:** Some businesses operate in multiple countries with strict data sovereignty laws. They can store sensitive data in private clouds located in specific geographic locations while leveraging public cloud resources for non-sensitive workloads.

Examples of Hybrid Cloud Providers:

- **AWS Outposts**: AWS offers hybrid cloud capabilities with **AWS Outposts**, allowing organizations to extend their on-premises data centers with AWS hardware and services.

- **Microsoft Azure Arc**: Azure Arc enables organizations to manage resources across hybrid and multi-cloud environments. It provides a consistent management experience for both on-premises and cloud workloads.

- **Google Anthos**: Anthos by Google enables organizations to manage their applications across multiple clouds, including public and private cloud environments, using a unified management platform.

Advantages of Hybrid Cloud:

- **Best of Both Worlds**: Organizations can leverage the scalability and cost-effectiveness of public clouds while maintaining the security and control of private clouds for critical workloads.

- **Cost Efficiency**: Hybrid clouds allow businesses to scale dynamically, using public cloud resources when needed and avoiding the expense of private cloud infrastructure when possible.

- **Agility and Flexibility**: Organizations can quickly respond to changing business needs by moving workloads between clouds as necessary.

Disadvantages of Hybrid Cloud:

- **Complexity**: Managing both private and public clouds can be complex, especially when it comes to data integration, security, and compliance.

- **Integration Challenges**: Achieving seamless integration between private and public clouds requires advanced infrastructure and careful planning, which can pose technical challenges for some organizations.

Practical Project

Now that you understand the differences and use cases of public, private, and hybrid clouds, it's time to implement a hybrid cloud solution. For this project, we will set up a hybrid environment using **AWS** (public cloud) and your own **private infrastructure** (which could be a virtualized environment, an on-premises server, or another private cloud setup).

Steps to Set Up a Hybrid Cloud Solution:

1. **Create an AWS Account**: If you don't already have one, sign up for an AWS free-tier account.

2. **Set Up a Virtual Private Network (VPN)**: Use AWS **VPN Gateway** to create a secure VPN connection between your private data center or virtual environment and AWS. This enables secure communication between the two clouds.

3. **Launch EC2 Instance on AWS**: Set up a basic EC2 instance on AWS and configure it to interact with your private infrastructure.

4. **Configure Private Cloud Infrastructure**: Set up your private cloud environment (whether it's a VMware-based private cloud or another solution). Ensure that it is connected to AWS via the VPN.

5. **Deploy Applications in Both Environments**: Deploy a simple web application on both your private infrastructure and AWS EC2 instance, ensuring they can communicate via the VPN.

Conclusion

Choosing the right cloud deployment model—**public**, **private**, or **hybrid**—depends on the specific needs and priorities of an organization. Public clouds offer scalability and cost efficiency, private clouds provide control and security, while hybrid clouds offer the flexibility to take advantage of both worlds. By understanding these deployment models, organizations can optimize their IT infrastructure for performance, cost, and security, and confidently embrace the future of cloud computing.

CHAPTER 4: SECURITY AND COMPLIANCE IN CLOUD COMPUTING

Why Cloud Security Matters

Security in the cloud is often considered one of the most crucial aspects of cloud computing, and for good reason. As businesses increasingly move their critical data and applications to cloud environments, the risk of potential breaches, data loss, and other security incidents escalates. However, understanding cloud security requires a more nuanced view. Unlike traditional on-premises infrastructure, the cloud presents unique challenges and opportunities when it comes to safeguarding sensitive data.

To break it down into digestible pieces, let's start by understanding the fundamental concepts of security in the cloud.

Cloud Security Analogy: The Bank Vault

Imagine you have important documents that you want to keep safe. You could store them in a locked filing cabinet in your office, or you could use a secure bank vault. Both options would keep your documents safe, but the way the security measures are implemented and the level of access granted will vary.

- **Your office filing cabinet** represents traditional IT security. The physical infrastructure (your filing cabinet) is in your control, and you manage the keys (or passwords) to that security. But, if something were to happen to the filing cabinet (e.g., a fire or theft), the documents could be compromised.

- **The bank vault** represents the cloud. A bank vault is professionally managed by security experts who ensure that it is protected from a variety of threats, like unauthorized access, theft, and natural disasters. You still maintain access to your documents, but you trust the bank (the cloud provider) to handle the physical security, ensure redundancy, and ensure the vault is equipped with state-of-the-art measures.

In this analogy, **cloud security** is the set of protocols, encryption, and access control mechanisms the cloud provider implements to ensure that your data stays safe, and only authorized users can access it.

Security and Shared Responsibility Model

Cloud computing introduces the concept of a **shared responsibility model**. This model clearly outlines the security roles and responsibilities between cloud providers (e.g., AWS, Azure, Google Cloud) and their customers (businesses and developers).

- **Cloud Providers' Responsibility**: The provider is responsible for securing the infrastructure, including physical hardware, network security, and ensuring the availability of services.

- **Customers' Responsibility**: As customers, businesses must protect their data, applications, and ensure proper user access control. This includes configuring the security settings, monitoring usage, and maintaining data encryption.

For example, if you're using AWS, they are responsible for securing the physical data centers and network infrastructure, but you, as a customer, must ensure that the data you store is encrypted and that only authorized personnel can access it.

Common Cloud Security Challenges

While the cloud offers robust security frameworks, it also comes with its own set of challenges. These challenges arise from both the nature of cloud computing and the way users interact with it.

1. Data Breaches

A **data breach** occurs when unauthorized individuals or entities gain access to sensitive information. The biggest concern when moving data to the cloud is the risk of external threats. The cloud is inherently accessible from anywhere, meaning that data stored in the cloud is at risk from cybercriminals, hackers, and even rogue insiders.

- **Targeted Attacks**: Cybercriminals often target cloud services due to the large volume of valuable data stored within them. These attacks can involve phishing, exploiting vulnerabilities in cloud software, or brute-forcing access to accounts.

- **Inadequate Encryption**: Without proper encryption, data is stored in an unprotected state, making it vulnerable to unauthorized access. In the event of a breach, unencrypted data is much easier to exploit.

Real-World Example: The **Capital One** data breach in 2019 involved a misconfigured firewall in their AWS environment. Hackers exploited this misconfiguration to access sensitive data, including personal information of over 100 million customers. Proper encryption and security configuration could have potentially prevented or minimized the breach.

2. Access Control

Access control refers to the process of ensuring that only authorized users can access specific resources, applications, or data. Mismanagement of access control is a critical security issue in cloud environments.

- **Over-Permissioned Users**: When users are given more access than they need, the chances of a breach increase. For example, a user might accidentally expose sensitive data or be targeted by an attacker due to unnecessary access permissions.

- **Inadequate Role-Based Access Control (RBAC)**: Without proper role-based access control (RBAC), users might be able to access parts of the cloud infrastructure that they shouldn't, which can lead to data leaks or misuse.

Real-World Example: In 2017, a cloud database owned by **Verizon** was left publicly accessible due to misconfigured access controls. The database contained the personal data of millions of customers. The breach was avoidable had proper RBAC and network access controls been in place.

3. Lack of Visibility and Monitoring

Cloud environments can be complex, and organizations often struggle to maintain visibility into their cloud infrastructure. A lack of visibility makes it difficult to detect and respond to security incidents in real time.

- **Monitoring Tools**: While cloud providers offer monitoring solutions like AWS **CloudTrail** and **Google Cloud Audit Logs**, the onus is on the customer to configure and properly use these tools to detect unusual activities.

- **Shared Responsibility**: While the cloud provider manages the infrastructure, it's the responsibility of the customer to implement proper logging, monitoring, and alerting for suspicious activities.

Security Solutions from Cloud Providers: How AWS, GCP, and Azure Ensure Security

All major cloud providers, including AWS, Google Cloud, and Microsoft Azure, have invested heavily in security to ensure their services are resilient against potential threats. Let's break down the key security features provided by these platforms.

1. AWS (Amazon Web Services)

AWS is a leader in the cloud space and offers a wide array of security solutions designed to help customers protect their data and applications.

- **Identity and Access Management (IAM)**: AWS IAM allows you to define roles and permissions for users within your AWS environment. You can control who can access specific resources and what actions they can perform, ensuring proper access control.

- **Encryption**: AWS provides several encryption options for securing data both at rest (e.g., **S3 encryption**) and in transit (e.g., **SSL/TLS**). AWS Key Management Service (KMS) enables you to manage and control encryption keys.

- **Security Groups and Network Access Control Lists (ACLs)**: AWS allows you to create virtual firewalls to control inbound and outbound traffic to your EC2 instances. By using security groups and ACLs, you can restrict access to your instances based on IP addresses, port numbers, and protocols.

2. Google Cloud Platform (GCP)

Google Cloud is known for its strong security foundation, with features that focus on automation, transparency, and compliance.

- **Cloud Identity & Access Management (IAM)**: GCP allows you to define roles and permissions for users and resources, enabling precise control over who can access which resources.

- **Google Cloud Key Management**: Google provides a robust set of encryption tools, such as **Google Cloud Key Management**, which allows organizations to create, manage, and rotate encryption keys for data stored on Google Cloud.

- **Private Google Access**: For enhanced security, GCP offers private Google access, enabling organizations to access Google services securely over a private network rather than through the public internet.

3. Microsoft Azure

Microsoft Azure is a favorite among enterprises, offering a rich set of tools that help businesses secure their data and applications.

- **Azure Active Directory (Azure AD)**: Azure AD is a cloud-based identity management solution that allows for role-based access control and seamless integration with on-premises Active Directory.

- **Azure Security Center**: This tool provides unified security management and threat protection across hybrid cloud environments. Azure Security Center offers recommendations, threat detection, and security assessments to ensure the integrity of your resources.

- **Encryption**: Azure provides data encryption both in transit and at rest. With **Azure Storage Service Encryption** and **Azure Key Vault**, you can ensure that your sensitive data is protected.

Practical Project: Implement Encryption for a Cloud-Based App and Set Up Access Control

Now that we've explored the importance of cloud security and how major cloud providers handle security, it's time to put this knowledge into practice. This project will walk you through encrypting data and setting up access control for a cloud-based web application hosted on AWS.

Step 1: Set Up an AWS EC2 Instance

To begin, launch an EC2 instance using a basic Amazon Linux AMI. You'll use this EC2 instance to host your web application.

1. **Launch EC2**: Follow the standard procedure for launching an EC2 instance on AWS. Ensure that you select a free-tier eligible instance, such as the **t2.micro** instance.

2. **Access EC2**: Once the instance is up and running, connect to it using SSH.

Step 2: Install Apache and PHP

On your EC2 instance, install Apache and PHP to host a simple web application:

bash

```
sudo yum update -y
sudo yum install -y httpd
sudo yum install -y php
```

Start the Apache service:

bash

```
sudo systemctl start httpd
```

Step 3: Encrypt Data Using AWS KMS

In this step, we'll encrypt data using AWS Key Management Service (KMS).

1. **Create a Key in AWS KMS**: In the AWS Management Console, navigate to **AWS KMS** and create a new encryption key.

2. **Encrypt Data**: Use the AWS SDK for PHP to encrypt sensitive data before it's stored in your database. Below is an example PHP code snippet for encrypting text:

php

```php
<?php
// Load AWS SDK for PHP
require 'vendor/autoload.php';

use Aws\Kms\KmsClient;
use Aws\Exception\AwsException;

$client = new KmsClient([
    'version' => 'latest',
    'region' => 'us-east-1'
]);

try {
    $result = $client->encrypt([
        'KeyId' => 'your-key-id',
        'Plaintext' => 'SensitiveData'
    ]);
```

```
// Get the encrypted data
$encrypted = base64_encode($result['CiphertextBlob']);
echo "Encrypted data: $encrypted";
} catch (AwsException $e) {
echo "Error encrypting data: " . $e->getMessage();
}
?>
```

Step 4: Set Up Access Control Using IAM

1. **Create an IAM Role**: In AWS IAM, create a new role with appropriate permissions for accessing the EC2 instance and using KMS for encryption.

2. **Attach the Role to EC2 Instance**: After creating the IAM role, assign it to the EC2 instance you launched earlier.

3. **Set Permissions for Access**: Ensure that only authorized users can access the sensitive data by configuring IAM policies with **least privilege** access.

Step 5: Testing the Security Features

To test your encryption and access control settings:

1. Try storing unencrypted data on the server to verify that it's rejected.

2. Test accessing the encrypted data by calling the decryption function, ensuring only users with appropriate access can decrypt the information.

Conclusion

Cloud security is a multifaceted discipline that requires a deep understanding of infrastructure, encryption, identity management, and access control. By leveraging the security solutions offered by AWS, GCP, and Azure, businesses can ensure their cloud environments are resilient to potential threats. Through proper configuration, monitoring, and adherence to security best practices, organizations can confidently embrace the cloud while protecting their sensitive data. The practical project in this chapter shows you how to apply these concepts by implementing encryption and access control, key elements of cloud security.

CHAPTER 5: CLOUD STORAGE AND DATA MANAGEMENT

Introduction to Cloud Storage: Types of Cloud Storage—Block, File, and Object Storage

Cloud storage is one of the foundational services that has enabled businesses to transition from traditional on-premises infrastructure to the cloud. It offers flexible, scalable, and cost-effective solutions for storing and managing data. Cloud storage is essentially a service that allows you to store data remotely in a way that is accessible from anywhere, as long as there is an internet connection.

Unlike traditional storage solutions that rely on physical hardware, cloud storage is virtualized and hosted on the infrastructure of cloud service providers like AWS, Google Cloud, and Microsoft Azure. These providers offer different types of storage options, each designed to meet specific use cases. Understanding the differences between block, file, and object storage is essential for effectively managing your data in the cloud.

1. Block Storage

Block storage is the most commonly used storage type in cloud environments when high-performance and low-latency access to data is required. It divides the data into blocks and stores each block as a separate unit. Each block has a unique address, which allows data to be retrieved quickly and efficiently. Block storage is ideal for applications that require high-speed access, such as databases and virtual machines (VMs).

In block storage, the data is presented to the user as raw storage. The user is responsible for managing the file system, directories, and data formatting. This gives users a higher level of control over the data and its structure.

USE CASES FOR BLOCK STORAGE:

- **Databases**: Block storage is ideal for database management systems like MySQL, PostgreSQL, and SQL Server. It provides the low-latency and high-throughput required for database operations.

- **Virtual Machines (VMs)**: Block storage is often used to store virtual disks associated with VMs. It allows VMs to have persistent storage that can be quickly read from and written to.

POPULAR PROVIDERS OF BLOCK STORAGE:

- **AWS EBS (Elastic Block Store)**: AWS provides scalable block storage for EC2 instances, allowing businesses to easily attach storage volumes to instances. AWS EBS is designed for high availability and low-latency access.

- **Google Persistent Disk**: Google Cloud offers **Persistent Disks**, which provide block storage for Google Compute Engine instances. They are highly durable and can be resized dynamically.

- **Azure Managed Disks**: Microsoft Azure offers **Managed Disks**, which provide durable and scalable block storage for Azure VMs.

2. File Storage

File storage refers to a system that stores and manages data in the form of files and directories, much like traditional file systems found on local machines. In a cloud environment, file storage allows multiple clients to access files over a network, making it ideal for applications that require shared access to data, such as collaborative document management or file-sharing applications.

File storage typically supports protocols like **NFS (Network File System)** or **SMB (Server Message Block)**, which are commonly used for accessing and managing files in a distributed manner. It is ideal for storing documents, images, videos, and other files that need to be organized hierarchically.

USE CASES FOR FILE STORAGE:

- **File Sharing**: File storage is commonly used in environments where multiple users need to collaborate on documents or media files. Think of a company's shared network drive where employees access files.

- **Backup and Archiving**: File storage systems are ideal for long-term data storage, backup, and archiving, where easy retrieval of files is essential.

Popular Providers of File Storage:

- **AWS EFS (Elastic File System)**: AWS offers EFS, a fully managed file storage service that supports NFS for Linux-based instances. EFS automatically scales to accommodate growing workloads, making it suitable for big data analytics and web content management.

- **Google Cloud Filestore**: Google Cloud offers Filestore, a fully managed file storage service for applications that require file storage, such as databases and content management systems.

- **Azure Files**: Microsoft Azure provides **Azure Files**, which offers fully managed file shares accessible via SMB. It's useful for migrating on-premises applications to the cloud.

3. Object Storage

Object storage is a storage architecture that manages data as objects rather than files or blocks. An object is a data unit that includes the data itself, metadata (data about the data), and a unique identifier (object key). This storage model is highly scalable and is designed to handle large amounts of unstructured data, such as backups, media files, logs, and big data.

Object storage is ideal for use cases where scalability, durability, and cost-efficiency are key factors. Object storage systems are highly distributed, meaning they spread the data across multiple servers or data centers, ensuring redundancy and availability.

USE CASES FOR OBJECT STORAGE:

- **Backup and Archiving**: Object storage is commonly used for long-term backups and archives, especially for large data sets.

- **Big Data and Analytics**: Object storage is perfect for storing the large volumes of unstructured data that are often processed in big data and machine learning workflows.

- **Content Distribution**: Services like media streaming and content delivery networks (CDNs) use object storage to deliver large files, such as video and images, efficiently.

POPULAR PROVIDERS OF OBJECT STORAGE:

- **AWS S3 (Simple Storage Service)**: Amazon S3 is one of the most popular object storage services. It provides scalable storage for a wide variety of use cases, including backups, archives, and content distribution. It also integrates with other AWS services, such as EC2 and Lambda.

- **Google Cloud Storage**: Google Cloud Storage offers object storage with high durability and low latency. It provides different storage classes, such as Standard and Nearline, for various use cases.

- **Azure Blob Storage**: Azure Blob Storage is Microsoft's object storage solution. It is highly scalable and integrates with many Azure services. Azure Blob Storage is often used for unstructured data, including media, logs, and backups.

Managing Data in the Cloud: Understanding Scalability, Backups, and Disaster Recovery

One of the most compelling reasons businesses move to the cloud is the ability to scale their storage needs efficiently and effectively. Cloud storage services provide the scalability, flexibility, and reliability needed to manage growing amounts of data while maintaining high availability. Let's dive into how scalability, backups, and disaster recovery work in cloud storage.

1. Scalability in Cloud Storage

Scalability refers to the ability to quickly and easily scale up or scale down storage resources according to your needs. Cloud storage is inherently scalable, meaning you don't have to worry about running out of space or overpaying for unused storage.

- **Vertical Scalability**: Vertical scaling involves adding more resources to your existing storage unit. For example, increasing the size of a disk or storage volume on an EC2 instance.

- **Horizontal Scalability**: Horizontal scaling involves adding more storage units or services to handle additional data. For example, adding more object storage buckets or file shares to handle growing data.

Cloud providers offer solutions that allow businesses to scale quickly and cost-effectively, ensuring they only pay for what they use.

Example: In AWS, **S3** provides virtually unlimited storage capacity, allowing users to scale their storage as needed without worrying about hardware limitations. AWS also offers **Elastic File System (EFS)**, which automatically grows and shrinks as files are added or removed.

2. Backup and Archiving in Cloud Storage

Cloud storage provides an effective solution for backing up data. Cloud backup services ensure that your data is consistently saved and available, even in the case of data loss or corruption. Many cloud storage providers offer automated backup services, so you can schedule regular backups without manual intervention.

Cloud backups are typically stored in multiple data centers, ensuring redundancy and availability. Additionally, cloud backups can be stored in different tiers, allowing businesses to optimize their backup strategies based on their needs for speed and cost.

- **Automated Backup**: Providers like AWS S3 allow users to automatically back up data by using services such as **AWS Backup** or **S3 Glacier** for long-term archival storage.

- **Data Versioning**: Many cloud services provide versioning capabilities, allowing you to keep track of different versions of your data. For example, AWS S3 supports **Versioning**, which allows you to store multiple versions of an object.

3. Disaster Recovery in Cloud Storage

Disaster recovery (DR) is another key aspect of cloud storage management. A well-designed DR strategy ensures that critical data can be recovered quickly after an unexpected event, such as a natural disaster, cyberattack, or system failure.

- **Cross-Region Replication**: Most cloud providers offer cross-region replication, which copies your data across multiple geographic locations. This ensures that your data is available even if one region experiences downtime.

- **Failover Mechanisms**: Cloud storage systems often incorporate automatic failover, where traffic or requests are automatically rerouted to a backup system or region if the primary system fails.

Example: Google Cloud Storage supports **multi-region** and **dual-region** storage options, which automatically replicate your data across multiple regions for disaster recovery.

Practical Project: Uploading and Managing Files on AWS S3 or Google Cloud Storage

In this project, we will walk through the process of uploading, managing, and securing files on cloud storage using **AWS S3** and **Google Cloud Storage**. Both of these services are highly reliable and provide easy-to-use interfaces for managing files.

1. Using AWS S3

AWS S3 is an object storage service that allows you to store and manage large amounts of data, such as files, images, and backups. It is highly durable and integrates well with other AWS services.

STEPS TO UPLOAD AND MANAGE FILES ON AWS S3:

1. **Set Up an AWS Account**: Sign up for an AWS account if you haven't already.

2. **Create an S3 Bucket**: Go to the AWS Management Console and navigate to S3. Click "Create Bucket" and give it a unique name. Choose a region and configure options such as versioning and encryption.

3. **Upload Files to S3**: You can upload files directly through the AWS Console or using the AWS CLI.

bash

```
aws s3 cp yourfile.txt s3://your-bucket-name/
```

4. **Configure Bucket Policies**: Use **Bucket Policies** to set permissions for who can access the files in your S3 bucket. You can also set **IAM policies** for fine-grained access control.

5. **Enable Versioning**: Enable versioning to keep track of different versions of files stored in the bucket.

2. Using Google Cloud Storage

Google Cloud Storage offers highly scalable object storage. It integrates well with other Google Cloud services, such as Compute Engine and BigQuery.

Steps to upload and manage files on Google Cloud Storage:

1. **Set Up a Google Cloud Account**: Sign up for a Google Cloud account.

2. **Create a Storage Bucket**: Go to Google Cloud Console, navigate to the **Storage** section, and click "Create Bucket". Choose a globally unique name for your bucket.

3. **Upload Files to Google Cloud Storage**: You can upload files through the Google Cloud Console or use the gsutil command-line tool.

bash

```
gsutil cp yourfile.txt gs://your-bucket-name/
```

4. **Set Permissions**: Use **IAM & Admin** to set up user roles and permissions for the bucket. You can restrict access to certain users or groups.

5. **Enable Object Versioning**: Google Cloud Storage also supports versioning. To enable it, set the versioning option in the bucket settings.

Conclusion

Cloud storage and data management are critical components of any modern cloud infrastructure. By understanding the differences between block, file, and object storage, businesses can make informed decisions about how to store and manage their data effectively. Cloud providers like AWS, Google Cloud, and Microsoft Azure offer robust solutions that make data storage scalable, secure, and accessible. With the hands-on project in this chapter, you've gained the practical experience necessary to manage files and ensure data security in the cloud.

CHAPTER 6: CLOUD NETWORKING AND CONTENT DELIVERY

Basics of Cloud Networking: Connecting Different Cloud Resources

Cloud networking is the backbone of cloud infrastructure, enabling the communication and connectivity between various resources deployed within a cloud environment. The concept of cloud networking involves several key components, including virtual networks, subnets, routing tables, and gateways that ensure different cloud resources—whether virtual machines, databases, storage solutions, or web applications—can securely and efficiently interact with each other and the outside world.

Unlike traditional on-premises networks, cloud networking offers the flexibility to create, scale, and manage virtualized network components. These networks are highly configurable, allowing businesses to design sophisticated architectures that meet their specific requirements for security, scalability, and availability.

Key Concepts in Cloud Networking:

1. **Virtual Networks (VNet)**: A virtual network (VNet) is the primary building block of cloud networking. It allows resources like virtual machines (VMs), containers, and

databases to communicate with each other within the cloud infrastructure. VNets provide a logically isolated network in the cloud, akin to a traditional on-premises network.

In platforms like **AWS**, **Google Cloud**, and **Azure**, VNets can span across multiple Availability Zones or Regions, ensuring high availability and fault tolerance.

2. **Subnets**: Subnets are subdivisions within a virtual network that provide further segmentation of the network. Each subnet can be isolated with its own IP address range, making it possible to separate different types of resources (e.g., frontend, backend) for security and performance reasons.

3. **Internet Gateway (IGW)**: The internet gateway is responsible for allowing resources in a VNet to communicate with the internet. It ensures that virtual machines (VMs) and applications hosted in the cloud can access public-facing resources, such as APIs, web servers, and other services.

4. **NAT Gateway**: A Network Address Translation (NAT) gateway allows resources in private subnets to access the internet without exposing their private IP addresses. This feature is often used for backend applications that need to access public services but should not be directly exposed to the public internet.

5. **Route Tables**: Route tables define how network traffic should be directed between different subnets and external resources. A properly configured route table ensures that data packets reach their intended destination efficiently and securely.

6. **VPN and Direct Connect**: Cloud providers offer Virtual Private Network (VPN) solutions and dedicated connections

like AWS Direct Connect and Azure ExpressRoute. These enable organizations to extend their on-premises networks into the cloud, establishing secure, low-latency communication between cloud resources and on-premises systems.

Why Cloud Networking Matters

Cloud networking is integral to the performance, scalability, and security of cloud-based applications. By leveraging virtual networks, businesses can segment resources and apply fine-grained control over who can access which parts of the network. Furthermore, the flexibility to scale the network dynamically ensures that businesses can respond to fluctuating traffic demands, whether through network isolation, load balancing, or content delivery.

Cloud networks are also highly secure. For instance, security groups and network access control lists (NACLs) allow users to define strict rules about who can access certain resources. Combined with firewalls, these mechanisms help secure data and prevent unauthorized access to sensitive infrastructure.

Virtual Private Cloud (VPC): Creating Isolated Networks within the Cloud

A **Virtual Private Cloud (VPC)** is a virtual network dedicated to your cloud resources, providing complete control over your networking environment. It is an isolated network within the cloud, ensuring that your cloud resources can be segregated from other tenants' resources and that traffic between different resources can be managed securely.

Key Components of VPC:

1. **Private Subnets**: A VPC consists of one or more **private subnets**, which are only accessible within the VPC or through specific gateway configurations (such as VPNs or Direct Connect). These subnets typically house backend services or databases that don't need to be directly accessed by the public internet.

2. **Public Subnets**: Public subnets are used for resources like web servers or load balancers that need to be accessible from the internet. Resources in these subnets are typically exposed via **Elastic IPs** or public IP addresses and can be accessed directly by users.

3. **Internet Gateway (IGW)**: An Internet Gateway (IGW) enables a VPC to communicate with the outside world by routing traffic between the VPC and the internet. It is the entry point for all incoming and outgoing traffic to and from public-facing applications.

4. **VPC Peering**: VPC peering allows you to connect two VPCs, enabling resources in one VPC to access resources in another. This feature is particularly useful for businesses that operate in multiple regions or who need to connect different environments (such as dev and prod).

5. **VPC Flow Logs**: VPC Flow Logs capture detailed information about the traffic flowing through a VPC, such as source IP addresses, destination IP addresses, and the amount of data transferred. These logs are invaluable for troubleshooting, monitoring, and compliance auditing.

Creating a VPC on AWS

AWS VPC is highly customizable, allowing businesses to tailor their virtual network according to specific needs. Here's how you can set up a VPC:

1. **Access the VPC Dashboard**: Log in to the AWS Management Console, navigate to the VPC dashboard, and click "Create VPC."

2. **Define the Network Configuration**: You'll be prompted to define the IP address range for your VPC (in CIDR notation, such as 10.0.0.0/16). This range determines the address space for the VPC and the subnets within it.

3. **Create Subnets**: You can now create one or more subnets within your VPC. For instance, create a public subnet for a web server and a private subnet for a database. Ensure that each subnet has its own IP range.

4. **Configure the Internet Gateway**: Attach an Internet Gateway to your VPC to allow internet access for public-facing resources. You can also associate the gateway with specific route tables to ensure correct routing of internet traffic.

5. **Set Up Security**: Implement **security groups** and **network ACLs** to protect your resources from unauthorized access. You can configure inbound and outbound traffic rules for each resource in the VPC.

Content Delivery Networks (CDN): How CDNs Speed Up Content Delivery Using Cloud Networks

A **Content Delivery Network (CDN)** is a distributed network of servers strategically placed in different geographical locations to serve content to users more efficiently. CDNs are designed to reduce latency and increase content delivery speeds by caching content closer to the end-user, which results in faster load times and better performance for websites and applications.

CDNs are particularly beneficial for high-traffic websites, streaming platforms, and globally distributed applications. By serving content from servers that are geographically closer to the user, CDNs help reduce the distance that data has to travel, lowering latency and improving user experience.

How CDNs Work:

1. **Content Caching**: The CDN caches static content—such as images, videos, JavaScript files, and HTML—on multiple edge servers located around the world. When a user requests content, the CDN server closest to the user's location serves the cached version, significantly reducing the time it takes for the content to load.

2. **Load Balancing**: CDNs distribute traffic across multiple servers to balance the load, preventing any single server from being overwhelmed. This process also helps to ensure high availability, even during periods of peak traffic.

3. **Dynamic Content Delivery**: CDNs can also accelerate dynamic content delivery by using technologies like **Anycast** routing, where the nearest data center responds to user

requests for dynamic content. Some CDNs, such as **Akamai** and **Cloudflare**, offer edge computing capabilities to process dynamic content at the edge before serving it to users.

Benefits of CDNs:

- **Improved Website Performance**: By reducing latency, CDNs enable faster page load times and a better overall user experience.

- **Scalability**: CDNs can handle large amounts of traffic by distributing content across multiple locations, ensuring that a website or application remains responsive during traffic spikes.

- **Reliability**: CDNs provide fault tolerance by replicating content across multiple servers. If one server or region fails, traffic is automatically routed to the next available server, reducing downtime.

- **Security**: CDNs provide security features such as DDoS protection, secure sockets layer (SSL) encryption, and web application firewalls to protect websites from cyber threats.

Popular CDN Providers:

- **AWS CloudFront**: AWS CloudFront is a global CDN that delivers content with low latency by caching content at edge locations around the world. It integrates seamlessly with other AWS services such as S3, EC2, and Lambda.

- **Google Cloud CDN**: Google's CDN leverages their global network infrastructure, offering low-latency content delivery for applications hosted on Google Cloud.

- **Cloudflare**: Cloudflare is one of the most widely used CDN providers, offering caching, load balancing, and security features for websites and applications.

Practical Project: Set Up a VPC and Deploy a Basic Application with CDN Using AWS or GCP

In this project, we will set up a **Virtual Private Cloud (VPC)** in AWS and deploy a basic web application. We will then configure a **Content Delivery Network (CDN)** using AWS CloudFront to ensure the application is delivered with low latency and high performance.

Step 1: Set Up the VPC in AWS

1. **Create the VPC**:

    o Log in to the **AWS Management Console** and navigate to the VPC dashboard.

    o Click "Create VPC" and define the CIDR block (e.g., 10.0.0.0/16).

    o Create both **public** and **private subnets** within your VPC.

2. **Attach an Internet Gateway**:

o   Navigate to the **Internet Gateway** section and create a new gateway.

o   Attach the gateway to your VPC to enable internet access for your public subnet.

3. **Set Up Route Tables**:

o   Create a **route table** that directs internet-bound traffic to the internet gateway for the public subnet.

4. **Launch EC2 Instance**:

o   In the **public subnet**, launch an EC2 instance (e.g., Ubuntu or Amazon Linux) to serve as your web server.

o   Install a web server (e.g., Apache or Nginx) on the instance and create a basic HTML webpage.

Step 2: Set Up AWS CloudFront for Content Delivery

1. **Create a CloudFront Distribution**:

o   Go to the **CloudFront** section of the AWS Management Console.

o   Click "Create Distribution" and choose the **Web** delivery method.

o   Set the **origin** as the S3 bucket or EC2 instance where your web content is hosted.

2. **Configure Cache Settings**:

o   Set the cache expiration time and other settings to control how content is cached at the edge locations.

3. **Enable SSL:**

   o   Use AWS **ACM (AWS Certificate Manager)** to provision a free SSL certificate for your domain and enable HTTPS for your CloudFront distribution.

4. **Point Your Domain to CloudFront:**

   o   Update your domain's DNS settings to point to the CloudFront distribution. This allows users to access your website via a faster and more secure delivery method.

Conclusion

Cloud networking and content delivery are fundamental to building scalable, secure, and high-performance cloud applications. By leveraging the power of **VPCs**, businesses can isolate and secure their resources, while **CDNs** accelerate content delivery, improving user experience worldwide. In this chapter, we've covered how to configure a VPC in AWS and deploy a basic web application, followed by setting up a CDN with AWS CloudFront. These techniques are critical for modern cloud architectures and empower organizations to deliver content efficiently and securely to a global audience.

CHAPTER 7: CLOUD COMPUTING IN THE REAL WORLD

Cloud computing has revolutionized various industries by providing scalable, flexible, and cost-effective solutions for business operations, data management, and application deployment. Its influence extends far beyond tech startups and large enterprises. As industries across the globe increasingly embrace the cloud, it has become clear that cloud technologies are not just reshaping how businesses operate, but also enabling entirely new business models, products, and services.

In this chapter, we will explore how cloud computing is being utilized across different sectors, including healthcare, manufacturing, finance, and retail. Each of these industries leverages cloud technologies to enhance efficiency, improve customer experiences, streamline operations, and scale rapidly. We will also dive into a practical project, building a cloud-based inventory management system for a retail store, to help solidify the concepts learned.

Cloud in Healthcare

The healthcare industry is undergoing a significant transformation, with cloud computing at the heart of this evolution. The need for efficient healthcare delivery, the rise of telemedicine, and the increasing volume of healthcare data have all led to the widespread adoption of cloud technologies. The cloud provides healthcare providers with flexible, secure, and scalable solutions for storing and managing patient data, improving patient outcomes, and optimizing clinical operations.

Key Benefits of Cloud Computing in Healthcare:

1. **Data Storage and Management:** Healthcare organizations generate vast amounts of data daily, including patient records, medical imaging, test results, and more. Storing and managing this data in a secure, efficient manner is crucial for maintaining continuity of care. Cloud storage solutions like **AWS S3**, **Google Cloud Storage**, and **Azure Blob Storage** enable healthcare organizations to store data in a centralized, accessible location. These services ensure data redundancy, high availability, and compliance with regulations like **HIPAA** (Health Insurance Portability and Accountability Act).

2. **Telemedicine and Remote Healthcare:** Cloud computing has played a pivotal role in the rise of **telemedicine**, allowing healthcare professionals to provide care to patients remotely. Platforms like **Zoom for Healthcare**, **Teladoc**, and **Amwell** rely on cloud technologies to facilitate secure, real-time video consultations between doctors and patients, as well as remote monitoring of patient vitals. By utilizing cloud infrastructure, healthcare providers can scale telemedicine services to meet patient demand and ensure seamless access to care.

3. **Collaboration and Data Sharing:** The cloud enables healthcare professionals to collaborate more effectively by providing a unified platform for sharing patient data. Tools

like **Google Workspace** and **Microsoft Teams** facilitate collaboration between physicians, specialists, and administrative staff, regardless of location. By storing patient information on cloud platforms, doctors can access up-to-date patient records in real-time, leading to more informed decision-making and better patient outcomes.

4. **Predictive Analytics and Machine Learning:** Cloud computing also enables the use of **predictive analytics** and **machine learning** to improve healthcare outcomes. Healthcare providers can use cloud-based analytics platforms like **Google AI Platform** or **AWS SageMaker** to analyze patient data and identify trends, predict disease outbreaks, and provide personalized care recommendations. Machine learning models can be trained on large datasets in the cloud, which is often more efficient than processing data on-premises.

Real-World Example:

In 2020, **Mount Sinai Health System** in New York leveraged cloud technologies to scale up its telemedicine services in response to the COVID-19 pandemic. The health system used AWS to build a robust telehealth platform that allowed doctors to remotely consult patients, manage appointments, and monitor patient data, all while maintaining HIPAA-compliant security protocols.

Cloud-Based Healthcare Applications:

- **Electronic Health Records (EHR):** Cloud-based EHR platforms, such as **Epic Systems** and **Cerner**, allow healthcare providers to store, manage, and access patient records in real-time. These platforms enhance collaboration, streamline workflows, and reduce the risk of errors in patient care.

- **Medical Imaging and Diagnostics**: Cloud storage services like **Google Cloud Healthcare API** allow healthcare providers to store and analyze medical images, such as X-rays and MRIs, ensuring that they are accessible to doctors and specialists across locations.

Cloud in Manufacturing

Manufacturing industries are increasingly using cloud technologies to enhance supply chain management, optimize factory operations, and streamline product development processes. With the rise of **Industry 4.0**, cloud computing is enabling manufacturers to integrate connected devices, sensors, and IoT (Internet of Things) technology into their production lines. This level of connectivity enhances operational efficiency, reduces downtime, and improves product quality.

Key Benefits of Cloud Computing in Manufacturing:

1. **IoT Integration and Smart Manufacturing:** The integration of **IoT devices** with cloud infrastructure allows manufacturers to collect real-time data from sensors embedded in machines, production lines, and other factory assets. Cloud platforms like **AWS IoT**, **Google Cloud IoT**, and **Microsoft Azure IoT** allow manufacturers to store, analyze, and act on this data in real-time. This process is known as **smart manufacturing**, where data-driven insights are used to monitor machine health, optimize production

schedules, and predict maintenance needs before failures occur.

2. **Supply Chain Management:** Cloud computing enables manufacturers to gain visibility across their entire supply chain by consolidating data from multiple sources, including suppliers, distributors, and customers. Cloud-based supply chain management platforms, such as **SAP Integrated Business Planning (IBP)** or **Oracle SCM Cloud**, allow organizations to monitor inventory levels, track shipments, and manage orders more effectively. With real-time data and analytics, manufacturers can optimize procurement, reduce excess inventory, and prevent stockouts.

3. **Collaborative Product Development:** Cloud-based platforms also enable collaboration across the product development lifecycle. Teams can work together on product design, simulations, and prototyping using cloud-based tools like **Autodesk Fusion 360** or **PTC Creo**. These tools allow designers and engineers to collaborate in real-time, no matter where they are located, speeding up time-to-market and improving product innovation.

4. **Predictive Maintenance and Equipment Monitoring:** Cloud computing allows manufacturers to monitor the health of equipment and machinery continuously. By collecting and analyzing data from sensors on factory floors, manufacturers can predict when equipment is likely to fail and take preventive measures before costly downtime occurs. Cloud-based solutions like **Uptake** and **GE Predix** use machine learning models to analyze equipment data and provide predictive insights for maintenance teams.

Real-World Example:

Siemens, a global manufacturing leader, utilizes cloud-based platforms to monitor its factory machines in real-time. By integrating IoT sensors with **AWS IoT** and cloud analytics, Siemens can track the health of its manufacturing equipment and schedule preventive maintenance to minimize downtime. This integration has significantly improved the efficiency of Siemens' production lines.

Cloud-Based Manufacturing Applications:

- **Enterprise Resource Planning (ERP)**: Cloud-based ERP systems like **SAP S/4HANA Cloud** and **Microsoft Dynamics 365** allow manufacturers to manage everything from procurement and inventory to production scheduling and accounting.

- **Digital Twins**: The cloud enables manufacturers to create **digital twins**, or virtual replicas, of physical assets. By simulating the behavior of machines and processes in a digital environment, manufacturers can test changes and predict outcomes without disrupting actual production.

Cloud in Finance and Retail: Cloud Solutions for Fraud Detection, Inventory Management, and E-Commerce

Cloud computing is reshaping the **finance** and **retail** industries by providing the scalability, security, and flexibility needed to handle large volumes of transactions, inventory, and customer data. Cloud-based solutions in these sectors not only enable operational efficiency but also improve customer experiences, enhance fraud detection, and facilitate data-driven decision-making.

Cloud in Finance:

1. **Fraud Detection and Prevention:** The financial industry is a prime target for cybercriminals, making fraud detection and prevention a top priority. Cloud platforms enable banks and financial institutions to deploy real-time fraud detection systems that analyze transaction data for suspicious patterns. Machine learning models powered by cloud services, such as **AWS Fraud Detector** or **Google Cloud AI**, can detect anomalies, flag high-risk transactions, and automatically trigger alerts or security actions to mitigate fraud.

2. **Data Security and Compliance:** Financial institutions are subject to stringent regulations like **PCI DSS (Payment Card Industry Data Security Standard)** and **GDPR (General Data Protection Regulation)**. Cloud providers offer secure infrastructure and tools to help organizations meet these compliance requirements. For example, **AWS CloudHSM** provides hardware-based key management to ensure secure encryption of sensitive data.

3. **Trading Platforms and Analytics:** Cloud computing has democratized access to financial trading platforms. Platforms like **E*TRADE** and **Robinhood** use cloud-based infrastructure to process high-frequency trading data, enabling real-time decision-making. Cloud-based analytics tools help financial institutions analyze market trends, optimize portfolios, and gain insights into customer behavior.

Cloud in Retail:

1. **E-commerce and Online Shopping:** Cloud computing is the foundation of modern e-commerce platforms, allowing retailers to scale rapidly during peak shopping periods. Cloud platforms like **Shopify**, **Magento**, and **BigCommerce** host retail websites and manage everything from product catalogs to payment processing and customer service. Retailers can leverage cloud-based infrastructure to ensure their websites remain operational during traffic surges (e.g., Black Friday or holiday seasons).

2. **Inventory Management and Supply Chain Optimization:** Cloud computing allows retailers to integrate their supply chains and manage inventory more efficiently. Solutions like **Oracle Retail Cloud** and **Microsoft Dynamics 365 Commerce** enable retailers to track inventory in real-time, manage stock levels across multiple locations, and predict demand to avoid overstocking or stockouts. This real-time data allows businesses to respond swiftly to changing market conditions.

3. **Customer Relationship Management (CRM):** Cloud-based CRM systems like **Salesforce** and **HubSpot** allow retailers to manage customer data and interactions more effectively. These platforms enable personalized marketing, customer service automation, and customer segmentation, which can lead to improved customer satisfaction and increased sales.

Real-World Example:

Walmart utilizes cloud technologies to optimize its supply chain, manage inventory, and enhance customer engagement. By integrating **Google Cloud** with its internal systems, Walmart can track inventory in real-time and respond to customer demand more efficiently. This has allowed the company to maintain its leadership in retail while ensuring that customers always have access to products when they need them.

Cloud-Based Finance and Retail Applications:

- **Customer Insights and Analytics**: Cloud-based data warehouses like **Google BigQuery** and **AWS Redshift** allow retailers and financial institutions to analyze customer data, understand purchasing patterns, and tailor offerings accordingly.

- **Payment Processing**: Cloud-based solutions like **Stripe** and **PayPal** enable secure and scalable payment processing for e-commerce platforms, making it easier for businesses to accept payments from around the world.

Practical Project: Build a Simple Cloud-Based Inventory Management System for a Retail Store

In this project, we'll build a simple cloud-based inventory management system for a retail store using **AWS** and **Amazon DynamoDB**. The goal is to help store owners track inventory, monitor stock levels, and receive notifications when products need to be restocked.

Step 1: Set Up AWS Services

1. **Create an AWS Account**: If you don't have an AWS account, sign up for one.

2. **Set Up DynamoDB:** Create a DynamoDB table for storing inventory items. Use the product name as the primary key and include attributes such as stock quantity, price, and description.

3. **Set Up Lambda Functions:** Use AWS Lambda to handle operations like adding inventory, updating stock levels, and generating alerts when stock is low.

4. **Create an API Gateway:** Set up an **API Gateway** to provide a RESTful interface for interacting with the DynamoDB table.

Step 2: Implement Inventory Management Features

1. **Add Inventory Items:** Use an API endpoint to allow users to add new items to the inventory, specifying the product name, quantity, and price.

2. **Update Stock Levels:** Implement an endpoint that updates the stock levels when products are sold or restocked.

3. **Low Stock Alert:** Create a Lambda function that checks inventory levels periodically. When stock reaches a predefined threshold (e.g., 10 units), the function will send an email alert to the store owner.

Step 3: Frontend and User Interface

1. **Create a Simple Web Interface:** Use **AWS Amplify** to host a simple frontend where the store owner can view inventory levels, add products, and update stock quantities.

2. **Display Inventory Data:** Use AWS Lambda functions to fetch data from DynamoDB and display it on the frontend in real-time.

Step 4: Deploy the System

1. **Deploy the Lambda Functions**: Once everything is set up, deploy the Lambda functions using AWS management tools.

2. **Test the System**: Test the inventory management system by adding products, updating stock, and ensuring that the low-stock alert works as expected.

Conclusion

Cloud computing has fundamentally transformed various industries, providing flexible, scalable, and secure solutions that enhance business operations and drive innovation. In healthcare, cloud technologies enable better patient care and remote services through telemedicine. In manufacturing, the cloud optimizes supply chains and factory operations through IoT integration and real-time data analytics. In finance and retail, the cloud powers fraud detection, customer engagement, and e-commerce solutions, allowing businesses to remain competitive and responsive to customer needs. Through the practical project in this chapter, you've gained hands-on experience building a cloud-based inventory management system, demonstrating the power of cloud technologies in action.

CHAPTER 8: INTRODUCTION TO CLOUD DEVELOPMENT TOOLS

Cloud development has emerged as a game-changing force in the world of software engineering, providing developers with the ability to create, deploy, and manage applications from anywhere in the world. With cloud computing, developers no longer need to worry about setting up complex development environments, managing dependencies, or maintaining local infrastructure. Instead, they can leverage cloud-based development environments that offer speed, scalability, and flexibility.

This chapter will delve into the tools and platforms that cloud providers offer for developers, such as **AWS Cloud9**, **Google Cloud Shell**, and **Azure Cloud Shell**. Additionally, we will guide you through choosing the right development tool for your project and provide a practical project where you'll set up a cloud development environment and deploy a basic web application. By the end of this chapter, you will have a comprehensive understanding of how to use cloud-based development tools to streamline your workflow and maximize productivity.

Cloud Development Platforms: Overview of Development Environments

Cloud-based development platforms are online Integrated Development Environments (IDEs) that allow developers to write, test, and deploy code directly from the cloud, eliminating the need for complex setups on local machines. These platforms provide an accessible and efficient way to develop software, collaborate with teams, and scale applications—all within the cloud. Let's explore some of the most popular cloud development platforms offered by major cloud providers: **AWS Cloud9**, **Google Cloud Shell**, and **Azure Cloud Shell**.

1. AWS Cloud9

AWS Cloud9 is Amazon Web Services' integrated development environment (IDE) that provides a rich, cloud-based environment for writing, running, and debugging code. Cloud9 is a fully managed IDE that allows you to work directly within the AWS ecosystem, eliminating the need to configure development environments on your local machine. It provides a seamless experience for creating web applications, serverless functions, and even AWS Lambda functions.

KEY FEATURES OF AWS CLOUD9:

- **Fully Managed IDE**: AWS Cloud9 provides a full-featured IDE that supports popular programming languages like Python, JavaScript, Java, and Ruby. It comes pre-installed with many tools and libraries, so developers don't need to manually install or configure them.

- **Integrated with AWS**: Cloud9 integrates directly with AWS services, allowing developers to manage AWS resources such as EC2 instances, Lambda functions, and S3 buckets without leaving the IDE.

- **Real-time Collaboration**: Cloud9 supports collaborative coding, enabling teams to work together on the same codebase in real-time. This is particularly useful for remote teams or developers working on open-source projects.

- **Terminal Access**: Cloud9 provides full terminal access, which is essential for managing cloud resources, interacting with databases, and running scripts.

WHY USE AWS CLOUD9?

- **Ease of Use**: With AWS Cloud9, you can quickly spin up an IDE environment that's ready to start coding. It eliminates the hassle of setting up development environments locally, which can often be time-consuming and prone to errors.

- **AWS Integration**: For projects hosted on AWS, Cloud9 offers deep integration with AWS services, making it easier to manage and deploy applications directly from the IDE.

- **Collaboration**: Cloud9's collaborative features make it ideal for teams, providing the ability to code together, review each other's work, and push changes directly from the IDE.

2. Google Cloud Shell

Google Cloud Shell is a browser-based, cloud-based development environment provided by Google Cloud Platform (GCP). Google Cloud Shell offers a rich set of tools for managing and deploying

Google Cloud resources, providing an efficient way to develop applications without the need for complex setups.

Key Features of Google Cloud Shell:

- **Pre-installed Development Tools**: Cloud Shell comes with many pre-installed development tools, including the **gcloud CLI**, **kubectl** (for Kubernetes), **Docker**, and **Git**, allowing developers to interact with GCP resources and deploy applications directly from the cloud.

- **Integrated with Google Cloud**: Cloud Shell provides native integration with Google Cloud, which makes it an excellent choice for developers building and managing Google Cloud-hosted applications. With access to Google Cloud APIs, developers can quickly deploy, test, and manage cloud resources such as GCE instances, Kubernetes clusters, and GCS buckets.

- **Persistent Storage**: Cloud Shell provides developers with 5GB of persistent storage, which allows them to store project files and configurations between sessions.

- **Web-based Editor**: Google Cloud Shell includes the **Cloud Shell Editor**, a browser-based code editor that supports multiple languages and integrates seamlessly with GCP services. Developers can write, test, and deploy code without leaving the browser.

WHY USE GOOGLE CLOUD SHELL?

- **No Setup Required**: With Google Cloud Shell, developers can start coding right away without worrying about environment setup. The platform is ready to use as soon as you access it.

- **Google Cloud Integration**: Google Cloud Shell is designed for developers who use Google Cloud Platform for their applications. The seamless integration with GCP resources ensures smooth workflows and better management of cloud infrastructure.

- **Built-in Tools**: Google Cloud Shell comes pre-equipped with a wide range of tools, saving developers time and effort by providing essential resources for coding, debugging, and deployment.

3. Azure Cloud Shell

Azure Cloud Shell is a cloud-based development environment from Microsoft's Azure platform. Azure Cloud Shell allows developers to manage Azure resources and build applications directly from the browser using a pre-configured shell environment.

KEY FEATURES OF AZURE CLOUD SHELL:

- **Pre-configured Environment**: Azure Cloud Shell comes pre-configured with the **Azure CLI**, **PowerShell**, **Docker**, and other essential tools that allow developers to manage Azure resources and perform development tasks without additional setup.

- **Integrated with Azure Services**: Cloud Shell seamlessly integrates with Azure services, making it ideal for developers building and deploying applications hosted on Azure. Developers can interact with Azure resources, such as **Azure**

Virtual Machines, **App Services**, and **Azure Functions**, directly from the Cloud Shell environment.

- **Persistent Storage**: Cloud Shell provides a persistent storage volume, ensuring that developers can store their scripts, files, and other project assets between sessions.

- **Browser-Based Editor**: Azure Cloud Shell features the **Visual Studio Code Editor**, a lightweight version of the popular desktop IDE. It supports syntax highlighting, debugging, and integration with Git repositories, making it ideal for web and cloud app development.

WHY USE AZURE CLOUD SHELL?

- **Azure Integration**: Azure Cloud Shell is built for developers working with Microsoft's cloud platform, and it offers seamless integration with Azure services, enabling easy management and deployment of resources.

- **Convenience**: With Azure Cloud Shell, developers don't need to worry about installing or configuring their development environments. The environment is pre-configured and ready to use as soon as you log in.

- **Persistent Storage**: The persistent storage feature makes it easy to store files and configurations, allowing developers to continue their work across sessions.

Choosing the Right Development Tool

Choosing the right cloud development tool depends on several factors, including the specific needs of the project, the cloud provider you're using, and the level of collaboration required. Here's a breakdown of how to choose the best development tool for your needs:

1. Consider Your Cloud Provider

The first factor to consider when choosing a cloud development tool is the cloud provider you're using. Each cloud provider—AWS, Google Cloud, and Azure—offers cloud development environments that are tightly integrated with their respective platforms. If your project is hosted on a specific cloud provider, using the corresponding development tool ensures a seamless workflow and better integration with the platform's resources.

- **Use AWS Cloud9** if your application is hosted on **AWS** or uses a lot of AWS-specific services like **EC2, Lambda**, and **S3**.

- **Use Google Cloud Shell** if your application relies heavily on **Google Cloud** services, such as **App Engine, BigQuery**, or **Kubernetes Engine**.

- **Use Azure Cloud Shell** if you are developing applications on **Microsoft Azure**, leveraging services like **Azure Functions, Azure Virtual Machines**, or **App Services**.

2. Evaluate Collaboration Needs

If you are working in a team or planning to collaborate with others, it's important to choose a tool that supports real-time collaboration. AWS Cloud9 supports collaborative development, allowing multiple developers to work on the same codebase simultaneously. This feature can be a game-changer for teams that need to work together on the same project.

Both **Google Cloud Shell** and **Azure Cloud Shell** support some level of collaboration, but **AWS Cloud9** has more advanced features for team collaboration, including built-in chat and the ability to share code with teammates.

3. Project Type

Consider the type of project you're building. Some development environments are better suited for specific use cases.

- **Use AWS Cloud9** for serverless applications, complex cloud-native apps, and applications that rely on multiple AWS services. AWS Cloud9's integration with **Lambda**, **DynamoDB**, and **EC2** makes it ideal for these use cases.

- **Use Google Cloud Shell** for projects that require heavy data analytics, machine learning, or real-time data processing with Google Cloud services like **BigQuery** and **AI Platform**.

- **Use Azure Cloud Shell** for Microsoft-centric applications, including those that integrate with **Azure Active Directory**, **SQL Database**, or **Windows Server-based apps**.

4. Language Support

All three platforms—**AWS Cloud9**, **Google Cloud Shell**, and **Azure Cloud Shell**—support a wide range of programming languages, including Python, JavaScript, Java, Ruby, and more. However, if your project is based on a specific language or framework, check the pre-configured environment of the development tool.

- **AWS Cloud9** supports many common programming languages and frameworks, including Node.js, Python, PHP, Ruby, and Go.

- **Google Cloud Shell** supports languages such as Python, Go, Node.js, and Java, with integration to Google Cloud-specific libraries for machine learning and data analytics.

- **Azure Cloud Shell** comes pre-configured with **PowerShell** and **Azure CLI** but also supports languages like Python, JavaScript, and .NET-based languages.

Practical Project: Set Up a Cloud Development Environment and Deploy a Basic App

For this practical project, we will walk you through setting up a cloud development environment using **AWS Cloud9** and deploying a basic web application.

Step 1: Setting Up AWS Cloud9

1. **Create an AWS Account**: If you don't have one, sign up for an AWS account.

2. **Launch AWS Cloud9**:

   o Navigate to the **AWS Cloud9** console and click on "Create Environment."

   o Name your environment (e.g., "WebApp-Dev"), choose the default instance type, and select an appropriate VPC.

3. **Access the Cloud9 IDE**: Once the environment is created, click on "Open IDE." This will open the Cloud9 IDE in your

browser, which comes pre-installed with essential tools like Node.js, Python, and Git.

Step 2: Setting Up the Basic Web Application

1. **Create a Node.js Application**:

   o Open the terminal in Cloud9 and create a new directory for your app:

bash

```
mkdir my-app && cd my-app
```

   o Initialize the project with:

bash

```
npm init -y
```

   o Install Express.js:

bash

```
npm install express
```

   o Create a basic app.js file:

javascript

```
const express = require('express');
const app = express();
const port = 3000;

app.get('/', (req, res) => {
```

```
res.send('Hello World!');
});

app.listen(port, () => {
  console.log(`App running at http://localhost:${port}`);
});
```

2. **Run the Application**: In the Cloud9 terminal, run your Node.js application:

bash

```
node app.js
```

Step 3: Deploying the Application

1. **Create an EC2 Instance**: To make your application publicly available, create an EC2 instance in the AWS console and attach an Elastic IP to it.

2. **Configure Security Group**: Ensure the EC2 instance's security group allows inbound traffic on port 3000.

3. **Deploy the App**: Upload your app.js to the EC2 instance and run it using SSH.

Step 4: Final Testing

Test the application by navigating to the Elastic IP address of your EC2 instance in a browser. You should see the message "Hello World!" displayed.

Conclusion

Cloud development tools like **AWS Cloud9**, **Google Cloud Shell**, and **Azure Cloud Shell** provide developers with powerful, scalable, and flexible environments for building, testing, and deploying applications. These tools enable you to focus on writing code and developing features, without the need for complex setup or infrastructure management. In this chapter, we've explored these platforms, highlighted their features, and guided you through a practical project, where you learned how to set up a cloud development environment and deploy a basic application. With these tools at your disposal, you can now leverage the full power of the cloud to streamline your development workflow and build innovative applications.

CHAPTER 9: PERFORMANCE OPTIMIZATION IN CLOUD APPLICATIONS

The cloud provides unparalleled flexibility and scalability, but these advantages come with their own challenges. As businesses increasingly rely on cloud applications for their operations, ensuring that these applications perform efficiently under various conditions is critical. Performance optimization involves a range of techniques aimed at improving the speed, responsiveness, and efficiency of cloud applications, ensuring they scale seamlessly and operate cost-effectively.

In this chapter, we will explore key concepts around cloud application performance, including understanding performance metrics, scaling strategies, and cost optimization techniques. We will also walk you through a practical project to help you set up auto-scaling and optimize your cloud application using platforms like AWS and Google Cloud Platform (GCP).

Understanding Cloud Performance Metrics

Performance optimization begins with understanding the key metrics that define how well an application runs in the cloud. By monitoring these metrics, you can gain insights into where bottlenecks might occur and take proactive measures to resolve them.

1. CPU Performance

The **CPU** (Central Processing Unit) is the brain of your cloud instance. It handles calculations, data processing, and task execution, so its performance is critical to the overall application speed and responsiveness. When applications experience high CPU usage, it often indicates that the application is under heavy load, possibly due to inefficient code, excessive computations, or inadequate resources.

KEY METRICS FOR CPU PERFORMANCE:

- **CPU Utilization**: This measures the percentage of CPU capacity being used. A high value (close to 100%) may indicate over-utilization and can lead to slower response times or application crashes.

- **CPU Load**: The number of processes waiting for CPU resources. A consistently high load value suggests that the application is under-provisioned for its workload.

- **CPU Throttling**: In the cloud, instances may be throttled when they exceed their allocated CPU credits, reducing performance temporarily.

HOW TO OPTIMIZE CPU PERFORMANCE:

- Scale your instances vertically (by increasing CPU capacity) or horizontally (by adding more instances).

- Optimize your application code to ensure it isn't performing unnecessary computations.

- Use auto-scaling to dynamically adjust CPU resources based on demand.

2. Memory (RAM) Performance

Memory, or **RAM**, is another critical factor that impacts the performance of cloud applications. Insufficient memory can result in slower processing times, increased latency, or application crashes. Applications that use memory inefficiently—such as by maintaining unnecessary data in memory—can cause significant performance degradation.

KEY METRICS FOR MEMORY PERFORMANCE:

- **Memory Utilization**: This metric shows how much of your instance's memory is being used. High memory usage may indicate that your application is demanding more memory than is available.

- **Memory Usage Spikes**: Sudden spikes in memory usage can lead to slow application performance or out-of-memory errors.

- **Memory Leaks**: A memory leak happens when an application continuously consumes memory without releasing it. Over time, this can cause resource exhaustion and slowdowns.

HOW TO OPTIMIZE MEMORY PERFORMANCE:

- Optimize application memory usage by ensuring that memory is released properly after each operation.

- Use managed services like **AWS Lambda** or **Google Cloud Functions** for event-driven applications that don't rely on constant memory use.

- Scale horizontally to distribute memory load across multiple instances or containers.

3. Network Performance

In cloud applications, **network performance** is a crucial factor in ensuring low latency and fast data transfer between instances, databases, and end-users. Network performance is particularly critical for applications that rely heavily on real-time data, such as streaming services or financial applications.

KEY METRICS FOR NETWORK PERFORMANCE:

- **Network Throughput**: The amount of data that can be transferred in a given period (measured in MBps or Gbps). Bottlenecks in throughput can lead to slow page loads or unresponsive applications.

- **Network Latency**: The time it takes for a data packet to travel from one point to another. High latency can degrade application performance, particularly for real-time applications.

- **Packet Loss**: The percentage of data packets that are lost during transmission. Packet loss can lead to communication failures and slow application performance.

HOW TO OPTIMIZE NETWORK PERFORMANCE:

- Optimize your network architecture to reduce the distance between your users and cloud resources, such as by using **content delivery networks (CDNs)** or **edge computing**.

- Use **Elastic Load Balancers (ELB)** or **Global Load Balancing** to distribute traffic across multiple availability zones or regions.

- Reduce dependencies on synchronous communication between microservices and use asynchronous methods, such as **message queues** or **event-driven architectures**.

4. Storage Performance

Storage performance is critical for applications that handle large amounts of data, such as file storage systems, databases, and big data applications. Slow storage performance can lead to delays in data retrieval, impacting the overall responsiveness of an application.

KEY METRICS FOR STORAGE PERFORMANCE:

- **Read/Write Latency**: The time it takes to read from or write to storage. High latency can significantly affect performance, especially for I/O-intensive applications.

- **Throughput**: The amount of data that can be read from or written to storage in a given time period. Insufficient throughput can cause delays in processing.

- **Input/Output Operations per Second (IOPS)**: This metric measures how many I/O operations can be performed per second. For applications that require high-performance storage, it's essential to have high IOPS.

How to Optimize Storage Performance:

- Choose the appropriate storage type (e.g., **EBS SSDs** for fast storage or **S3** for scalable object storage).

- Optimize data retrieval by minimizing the number of storage reads/writes, using techniques like **caching** and **data indexing**.

- Scale storage vertically or horizontally based on the volume of data being processed.

Scaling Cloud Applications: Autoscaling, Load Balancing, and Failover Strategies

Scaling cloud applications involves adjusting resources to accommodate varying levels of traffic, data, and workload. The cloud's ability to scale automatically, both vertically (increasing resource capacity) and horizontally (adding more resources), is one of its most powerful features. Scaling is not just about adding more instances; it also includes optimizing resource allocation, managing load balancing, and ensuring high availability.

1. Autoscaling

Autoscaling is the process of automatically adjusting the number of compute resources (instances, containers, etc.) based on traffic or load. This ensures that your application can handle spikes in traffic and reduce resources when demand is low, optimizing both performance and cost.

- **AWS Auto Scaling**: AWS allows you to configure autoscaling groups that automatically increase or decrease the number of EC2 instances based on predefined conditions, such as CPU utilization or memory usage.

- **Google Cloud Autoscaler**: Google Cloud provides **Instance Group Autoscaling**, which adjusts the size of an instance group based on load, ensuring optimal performance for applications hosted on Compute Engine.

- **Azure Autoscale**: Azure provides autoscaling features for both virtual machines and app services, allowing automatic scaling based on performance metrics such as CPU load or memory usage.

BEST PRACTICES FOR AUTOSCALING:

- Set appropriate thresholds for autoscaling policies, such as CPU or memory usage, to ensure resources scale appropriately.

- Test autoscaling configurations to ensure they perform as expected during traffic surges.

- Use **load balancers** to distribute incoming traffic across multiple instances or containers.

2. Load Balancing

Load balancing distributes incoming traffic across multiple servers or instances to prevent any single resource from being overwhelmed. This ensures high availability and optimal performance, especially during high traffic periods.

- **Elastic Load Balancer (ELB)** in AWS: ELB automatically distributes incoming application traffic across multiple targets (e.g., EC2 instances, containers, or IP addresses) to ensure no single instance is overburdened.

- **Google Cloud Load Balancing**: Google's global load balancing distributes user requests across multiple instances, regions, and data centers, minimizing latency and improving response times.

- **Azure Load Balancer**: Azure provides both internal and external load balancing solutions, ensuring high availability and distributing traffic evenly across resources.

BEST PRACTICES FOR LOAD BALANCING:

- Choose the appropriate load balancing algorithm (e.g., round-robin, least connections) based on your application needs.

- Use **health checks** to monitor the status of backend resources and ensure traffic is only directed to healthy instances.

- Integrate load balancing with **autoscaling** to ensure resources scale appropriately based on demand.

3. Failover Strategies

Failover strategies ensure that your cloud application remains available and resilient, even in the event of resource failure or unplanned downtime. Failover automatically reroutes traffic to healthy resources, minimizing downtime and disruption.

- **Multi-AZ and Multi-Region Failover**: By deploying resources in multiple availability zones (AZs) or regions, you can ensure that if one resource becomes unavailable, traffic is rerouted to another healthy instance or region.

- **AWS Route 53**: AWS Route 53 provides **DNS failover** capabilities, allowing traffic to be routed to a backup resource if the primary resource fails.

- **Google Cloud Failover**: Google Cloud provides **global HTTP(S) load balancing** with built-in failover capabilities to route traffic to healthy instances automatically.

BEST PRACTICES FOR FAILOVER:

- Implement multi-AZ or multi-region architectures to ensure redundancy.

- Use **backup databases** or data replication to ensure data availability in case of a failure.

- Regularly test your failover strategy to ensure it performs as expected during incidents.

Cost Optimization: Tips on Managing and Optimizing Cloud Expenses

While scaling and optimizing cloud application performance are essential, managing costs is just as critical. Cloud resources are typically billed based on usage, so optimizing your resources to align with actual demand is key to keeping your cloud costs under control.

1. Choose the Right Instance Types

Cloud providers offer a wide range of instance types tailored to different workloads. Whether you need compute-intensive, memory-intensive, or I/O-heavy instances, choosing the right instance type can significantly impact both performance and cost.

BEST PRACTICES:

- Regularly review your instance usage and choose instance types that match your application's needs.

- Consider using **spot instances** or **reserved instances** for workloads that can tolerate interruptions or that require long-term commitments.

2. Use Auto-scaling and Load Balancing Efficiently

Auto-scaling and load balancing not only improve performance but also help optimize costs. By dynamically adjusting the number of resources based on demand, you only pay for what you use.

BEST PRACTICES:

- Set up **scheduled scaling** to automatically scale resources based on predictable traffic patterns.

- Use **instance right-sizing** to ensure that your instances are appropriately sized for your workload.

3. Take Advantage of Managed Services

Managed services like **AWS Lambda, Google Cloud Functions,** and **Azure Functions** allow you to pay only for the actual execution time of your code, rather than for provisioned compute resources. These services provide a cost-effective solution for event-driven applications.

BEST PRACTICES:

- Migrate appropriate workloads to serverless computing to minimize idle time and reduce costs.

- Use **managed databases** like **Amazon RDS, Google Cloud SQL,** or **Azure SQL Database,** which offer built-in optimization features like automatic backups and scaling.

4. Leverage Cloud Storage and Caching Solutions

Storing data in the cloud can be costly, especially for high-volume applications. To reduce storage costs, leverage caching solutions like **Amazon CloudFront, Google Cloud CDN,** or **Azure CDN** to cache frequently accessed content closer to users. Additionally, use **object storage** (e.g., S3, Google Cloud Storage) for cost-effective long-term data storage.

BEST PRACTICES:

- Archive infrequently accessed data to lower-cost storage tiers, such as **AWS Glacier** or **Google Cloud Nearline**.

- Use **content delivery networks (CDNs)** to offload traffic from your servers and reduce bandwidth costs.

Practical Project: Set Up Auto-Scaling on AWS or GCP for a Web Application

In this practical project, we will set up auto-scaling for a simple web application using **AWS EC2** or **Google Compute Engine** (GCP). This will ensure that the application scales dynamically based on incoming traffic, helping to optimize both performance and cost.

Step 1: Set Up the Web Application

1. **Launch an EC2 Instance (AWS)** or **Compute Engine VM (GCP)** and install a web server (e.g., **Apache** or **Nginx**).

2. **Deploy a Simple Web App**: Upload your basic web application (e.g., a Node.js app) to the server.

Step 2: Configure Auto-Scaling

1. **AWS Auto-Scaling**:

   o Create an **Auto Scaling Group** and define the desired capacity, minimum, and maximum number of instances.

- o   Set up **CloudWatch Alarms** to trigger scaling actions based on CPU utilization or other metrics.

2. **GCP Auto-Scaling**:

- o   Create an **instance group** in Google Cloud and enable **auto-scaling** based on CPU utilization or other metrics.

Step 3: Test the Auto-Scaling Configuration

1. **Load Test**: Simulate high traffic using tools like **Apache JMeter** or **Gatling** and monitor how the application scales.

2. **Observe Scaling**: Watch as your instances automatically scale in response to traffic increases and decreases.

Conclusion

Performance optimization in cloud applications involves understanding key performance metrics such as CPU, memory, network, and storage, and applying strategies like autoscaling, load balancing, and failover to maintain efficiency and high availability. By following best practices for scaling and cost optimization, businesses can not only improve performance but also reduce unnecessary cloud expenses. The practical project in this chapter provided hands-on experience with setting up auto-scaling for a cloud-based web application, reinforcing the concepts learned throughout the chapter. Cloud computing offers the power and flexibility needed to build and maintain high-performing, cost-effective applications in today's dynamic, data-driven world.

CHAPTER 10: SERVERLESS COMPUTING: THE FUTURE OF CLOUD

Serverless computing is rapidly becoming the backbone of modern cloud applications, offering a revolutionary way to develop and deploy software. By abstracting the infrastructure layer, serverless computing eliminates the need for developers to manage servers, allowing them to focus solely on writing code. In this chapter, we will explore the concept of serverless computing, its benefits, and real-world use cases. Additionally, we will guide you through a practical project where you'll build a simple serverless function using **AWS Lambda** or **Azure Functions**.

What is Serverless?

At its core, **serverless computing** allows developers to build and run applications without managing any servers. While the term "serverless" can be misleading—since servers are still involved in executing the code—what it truly refers to is the abstraction of the underlying infrastructure. Serverless services allow you to deploy functions (small units of business logic) without worrying about server provisioning, scaling, or maintenance.

1. How Serverless Works

In traditional cloud computing, developers typically provision servers (virtual machines) to run their applications. This approach requires handling infrastructure provisioning, capacity planning, scaling, and maintaining the servers over time. The serverless model removes this responsibility by using event-driven functions that are executed on demand.

When a specific event occurs, such as an HTTP request, a file upload, or a database update, the serverless platform automatically spins up the necessary compute resources, runs the code, and then terminates the resources when the job is done. This means you pay only for the compute time used during the execution of the function, rather than for always-on resources.

2. Major Serverless Platforms

Several major cloud providers offer serverless computing platforms. Each of these platforms offers its own set of tools and services, making it important to understand which one best suits your project's needs.

- **AWS Lambda: AWS Lambda** is perhaps the most well-known serverless computing service. It allows you to run your code in response to events such as HTTP requests (via Amazon API Gateway), changes in data (via Amazon S3 or DynamoDB), or even direct invocations from other AWS services. Lambda is highly scalable and supports a variety of programming languages, including Node.js, Python, Java, and Go.

- **Google Cloud Functions: Google Cloud Functions** is Google's serverless solution, offering a similar service to

AWS Lambda. It is integrated with other Google Cloud services like **Cloud Pub/Sub**, **Google Cloud Storage**, and **Firebase**, allowing developers to trigger functions based on events in the Google Cloud ecosystem. It supports multiple languages, including JavaScript, Python, and Go.

- **Azure Functions: Azure Functions** is Microsoft's serverless computing offering, which is highly integrated into the Azure ecosystem. It supports multiple languages, including C#, JavaScript, Python, and Java. Azure Functions also integrates tightly with services like **Azure Blob Storage**, **Azure Service Bus**, and **Azure Event Grid**, enabling seamless event-driven workflows.

Each of these platforms offers an event-driven model where the function is triggered by specific actions or events, such as API calls, file uploads, database updates, or scheduled jobs. The primary difference between these platforms lies in the specific integrations, features, and language support they offer.

3. Event-Driven Architecture

At the heart of serverless computing is the **event-driven architecture**. In a serverless model, an event acts as the trigger for the execution of a function. Events can be anything from an HTTP request, a file being uploaded to storage, a database record being updated, or even time-based events like a cron job.

This approach allows applications to scale automatically in response to real-time data and external events. For example, when a user uploads an image to Amazon S3, an AWS Lambda function could automatically process the image (e.g., resizing, applying filters) and then store it back in S3.

Benefits of Serverless Computing: Cost-Effectiveness, Scalability, and Simplicity

Serverless computing provides numerous benefits, making it an attractive choice for modern cloud application development. The major advantages are cost-effectiveness, scalability, and simplicity.

1. Cost-Effectiveness

One of the most compelling benefits of serverless computing is its cost-effectiveness. With traditional server-based architectures, you must provision enough servers to handle peak loads, even though most of the time those servers may be underutilized. With serverless, you pay only for the actual compute time used by the functions, meaning that when there is no traffic or demand, you incur no charges.

- **Pay-per-Use**: You only pay for the compute time consumed by the function during execution, which means costs are directly proportional to usage. If your function runs for 100 milliseconds, you only pay for those 100 milliseconds of processing time.

- **No Idle Costs**: Unlike virtual machines or containers that run 24/7, serverless functions do not incur costs when idle. This makes serverless computing ideal for applications with unpredictable traffic patterns or sporadic workloads.

2. Scalability

Serverless computing excels at automatically scaling based on demand. The cloud platform manages the scaling of compute resources for you, ensuring that your application can handle traffic spikes without requiring manual intervention.

- **Automatic Scaling**: Serverless platforms automatically scale resources up or down based on the volume of incoming events. For example, if an API endpoint triggers a function and it suddenly receives millions of requests, the platform will dynamically scale the number of function executions to meet the demand.

- **Effortless Management**: Since the platform handles scaling for you, there's no need to worry about provisioning or managing servers to handle different traffic levels. This enables developers to focus on building the application instead of worrying about infrastructure.

3. Simplified Development and Operations

Serverless computing abstracts away much of the complexity involved in managing infrastructure, making development and operations much simpler.

- **No Server Management**: With serverless computing, developers do not need to provision, configure, or manage servers. The cloud provider handles all of the infrastructure management, allowing developers to focus solely on writing business logic.

- **Event-Driven**: Serverless architectures are inherently event-driven, which means you can easily build decoupled systems that respond to real-time events. This allows for faster development cycles and greater flexibility.

- **Reduced Operational Overhead**: Serverless computing eliminates the need to manage the underlying infrastructure, such as load balancing, auto-scaling, and server maintenance. This drastically reduces the operational overhead typically associated with cloud applications.

4. Faster Time to Market

Since serverless platforms handle infrastructure concerns, developers can focus solely on writing code. The rapid development cycle made possible by serverless allows teams to quickly prototype and deploy applications, significantly reducing time-to-market.

- **Easier to Deploy**: Serverless functions are typically deployed with a single click or command. Developers do not need to worry about server provisioning or network configuration.

- **Faster Iteration**: Serverless computing allows for continuous deployment and integration. Developers can update and deploy new versions of a function with minimal downtime and without the complexity of managing servers.

Real-World Serverless Applications: Building Small-Scale Apps with Serverless Functions

Serverless computing is ideal for a wide variety of use cases, especially for small to medium-sized applications, event-driven workloads, and applications with unpredictable traffic patterns. Here are a few real-world examples of serverless applications:

1. Real-Time Image Processing

A common use case for serverless computing is **real-time image processing**. For instance, a photo-sharing app could use serverless functions to automatically resize or apply filters to user-uploaded images.

- **How it Works**: When a user uploads an image to a cloud storage service (e.g., **AWS S3**), it triggers an event that invokes a serverless function (e.g., **AWS Lambda**). The function processes the image (resizing, compressing, etc.) and stores the processed image back in the storage service.

- **Advantages**: Serverless computing enables automatic scaling to handle high numbers of concurrent image uploads without needing to provision servers. You only pay for the compute time when images are processed.

2. Real-Time Data Processing

Serverless architectures are also well-suited for **real-time data processing** applications. For example, a financial service might use serverless functions to analyze real-time stock market data or process financial transactions.

- **How it Works**: The service receives real-time data from a stream (e.g., **AWS Kinesis** or **Google Cloud Pub/Sub**), which triggers a serverless function. The function processes the data, performs analysis, and stores the results in a database or sends notifications.

- **Advantages**: The serverless model allows you to process high volumes of data at scale, with low latency. The platform automatically scales based on the number of incoming data events, ensuring that the application can handle spikes in data volume.

3. API Backends

Serverless computing is an excellent choice for building **API backends**. By using cloud functions to handle HTTP requests, you can easily build RESTful APIs that scale automatically based on traffic.

- **How it Works**: When an HTTP request is made to an API endpoint (e.g., through **Amazon API Gateway, Google Cloud Endpoints**, or **Azure API Management**), the request triggers a serverless function (e.g., **AWS Lambda, Azure Functions**). The function processes the request and returns the response.

- **Advantages**: Serverless APIs are highly scalable and cost-effective, as you only pay for the actual requests processed by the function. The backend automatically scales in response to varying traffic levels.

Practical Project: Build a Simple Serverless Function Using AWS Lambda or Azure Functions

In this project, we will build a simple serverless function using **AWS Lambda** or **Azure Functions**. The goal of this project is to introduce you to the process of setting up, deploying, and testing a serverless function in a cloud environment.

Step 1: Set Up AWS Lambda

1. **Create an AWS Account**: If you don't have an AWS account, sign up for one at <u>AWS</u>.

2. **Create a Lambda Function**:

    o   Navigate to the **AWS Lambda** console and click "Create function."

    o   Choose the "Author from scratch" option, and select a runtime (e.g., Node.js, Python).

    o   Set up the function's basic configuration (e.g., function name, execution role).

3. **Write Code for the Function**: For this example, let's create a simple function that returns a greeting message.

javascript

```javascript
exports.handler = async (event) => {
  const name = event.queryStringParameters.name || 'World';
  const message = `Hello, ${name}!`;
  return {
    statusCode: 200,
    body: JSON.stringify({ message }),
  };
};
```

4. **Test the Lambda Function**:

    o   You can test the Lambda function directly within the AWS Lambda console. Click on "Test" and provide input, such as the name of the user to greet.

Step 2: Set Up API Gateway

1. **Create an API Gateway**:

   o In the **API Gateway** console, click "Create API."

   o Choose a **REST API** and configure it to trigger your Lambda function when an HTTP request is made to a specific endpoint.

2. **Deploy the API**:

   o Deploy the API to make it publicly accessible.

   o After deployment, you'll receive a URL that you can use to test your Lambda function via HTTP requests.

3. **Test the API**:

   o Using a tool like **Postman** or simply your browser, send a GET request to the API URL with a query parameter for the name (e.g., https://api-id.execute-api.region.amazonaws.com/hello?name=John).

   o You should see the response: {"message":"Hello, John!"}.

Step 3: Set Up Azure Functions

1. **Create an Azure Account**: Sign up for an Azure account at Azure.

2. **Create an Azure Function**:

   o Navigate to **Azure Functions** in the Azure portal and click "Create function."

- o   Select the runtime (e.g., JavaScript, Python) and configure your function.

3. **Write Code for the Function**: For the same greeting function, the code might look like this:

javascript

```
module.exports = async function (context, req) {
  const name = req.query.name || 'World';
  context.res = {
    body: `Hello, ${name}!`,
  };
};
```

4. **Test the Azure Function**:

- o   You can test the function directly from the Azure portal. Use the provided HTTP endpoint to send a GET request with the name query parameter.

Step 4: Test and Deploy

Once the function is set up, test it using the provided endpoints and ensure the responses are correct. If necessary, deploy the function and integrate it into your application or service.

Conclusion

Serverless computing represents the future of cloud-based application development by simplifying infrastructure management, reducing costs, and offering unparalleled scalability. By abstracting away the complexities of server management, serverless platforms like **AWS Lambda, Google Cloud Functions**, and **Azure Functions** allow developers to focus purely on writing code that responds to events.

This chapter has introduced you to the core concepts of serverless computing, provided real-world use cases, and guided you through a practical project that involves building a simple serverless function. With serverless platforms, developers can now create highly scalable, event-driven applications that only consume resources when needed—transforming how we approach cloud application development.

CHAPTER 11: DEVOPS AND CONTINUOUS INTEGRATION IN THE CLOUD

In the modern era of cloud computing, software development practices are constantly evolving to meet the demand for faster delivery, higher-quality applications, and more efficient workflows. **DevOps** is at the heart of this transformation, enabling development and operations teams to collaborate seamlessly. With the added complexity of cloud environments, DevOps practices have become even more crucial, particularly when combined with **Continuous Integration** (CI) and **Continuous Delivery** (CD).

In this chapter, we will provide an in-depth look at DevOps, its principles in cloud environments, and how continuous integration and delivery pipelines (CI/CD) are set up in the cloud. We'll also discuss key automation tools like Jenkins, CircleCI, and GitHub Actions and how they help streamline workflows in the cloud. Finally, we'll walk through a practical project where you'll set up a simple CI/CD pipeline on AWS, Google Cloud, or Azure.

What is DevOps?

DevOps is a cultural and technical movement that aims to improve the collaboration between development (Dev) and operations (Ops) teams. It emphasizes automation, monitoring, and fast feedback loops to ensure that software is delivered more efficiently and with higher quality.

Key Principles of DevOps:

1. **Collaboration Between Development and Operations**: DevOps aims to break down the silos between development teams (who write the code) and operations teams (who manage deployment and infrastructure). By fostering collaboration, DevOps encourages teams to work together throughout the entire application lifecycle—from coding to deployment and monitoring.

2. **Automation**: Automation is a cornerstone of DevOps. Repetitive tasks such as building, testing, and deploying applications are automated to reduce human errors, speed up processes, and increase consistency. Automation tools and scripts are used to handle everything from code integration to infrastructure provisioning and deployment.

3. **Continuous Integration and Continuous Delivery (CI/CD)**: CI/CD practices are the backbone of DevOps, enabling teams to frequently integrate code changes, run automated tests, and automatically deploy new versions of applications. This ensures that software is always in a deployable state and can be shipped quickly and reliably.

4. **Monitoring and Feedback**: DevOps also emphasizes monitoring applications in real-time to gather feedback. This allows teams to identify and address issues early, ensuring that applications remain healthy and that customers get a seamless experience. Monitoring tools help track performance metrics, logs, and errors.

5. **Infrastructure as Code (IaC)**: Infrastructure as Code is a key practice within DevOps that allows infrastructure to be provisioned and managed through code. With IaC, developers can manage infrastructure just as they would with application code, ensuring consistency across environments and reducing configuration drift.

DevOps in Cloud Environments:

Cloud computing has greatly enhanced DevOps practices by offering flexible, scalable, and easily configurable environments. Cloud providers like **AWS**, **Google Cloud**, and **Azure** provide a variety of tools and services that support DevOps workflows, making it easier to automate and scale infrastructure and application deployments. Cloud environments make it easier to implement **Infrastructure as Code (IaC)** and ensure that infrastructure is consistent across development, staging, and production environments.

The cloud offers dynamic scalability, which is crucial for DevOps. For example, with cloud-based infrastructure, DevOps teams can spin up test environments automatically as part of the CI/CD pipeline without needing to manage physical hardware.

Cloud CI/CD Pipelines: How to Set Up Continuous Integration and Delivery Pipelines in the Cloud

A **CI/CD pipeline** is an automated workflow that allows teams to deliver code changes faster and with more reliability. The pipeline typically consists of several stages that manage code integration, testing, and deployment.

Continuous Integration (CI)

Continuous Integration is the practice of frequently integrating code into a shared repository, where it is automatically tested to ensure it works as expected. The primary goal of CI is to detect integration issues early in the development cycle, allowing developers to address problems before they become costly.

Key stages of Continuous Integration include:

1. **Code Commit**: Developers write code and commit it to the shared repository (e.g., GitHub, GitLab).

2. **Build**: Once code is committed, the CI system automatically builds the application, compiling the code and ensuring that the application can be successfully built.

3. **Test**: After building, automated tests are run (unit tests, integration tests, etc.) to ensure the new changes haven't broken any existing functionality.

4. **Feedback**: If any issues are found during the build or test stages, feedback is provided to the developer immediately, allowing them to fix issues before the code is merged.

Continuous Delivery (CD)

Continuous Delivery extends CI by automating the deployment process. Once code passes all tests in the CI pipeline, it is automatically deployed to a staging or production environment. The goal of CD is to ensure that code can be released to production at any time, without manual intervention.

Key stages of Continuous Delivery include:

1. **Deployment**: After successful tests, the code is automatically deployed to a staging environment where it can be tested further.

2. **Production Release**: If the code is stable and has passed all tests, it is automatically deployed to the production environment, allowing teams to release new features quickly and reliably.

Setting Up CI/CD Pipelines in Cloud Platforms

Cloud platforms like AWS, GCP, and Azure provide native tools to set up and manage CI/CD pipelines. Below are some of the most widely used tools across these platforms:

- **AWS CodePipeline**: AWS provides **CodePipeline**, a fully managed CI/CD service that automates the build, test, and deployment of applications. It integrates with other AWS services such as **CodeCommit** (source code repository), **CodeBuild** (build service), and **CodeDeploy** (deployment service).

- **Google Cloud Build**: Google Cloud offers **Cloud Build**, which allows you to define and automate the CI/CD process using YAML configuration files. Cloud Build integrates with Google Cloud services and allows developers to trigger builds based on events from repositories like **GitHub** or **GitLab**.

- **Azure Pipelines**: Azure provides **Azure Pipelines**, which is part of the **Azure DevOps** suite. It supports both CI and CD for various languages and platforms, integrates with **GitHub**, and provides tools for testing, building, and deploying applications on Azure.

Automating Workflows: Using Tools Like Jenkins, CircleCI, and GitHub Actions in the Cloud

Automation is a central component of DevOps practices, and many cloud platforms provide tools to automate workflows and streamline the CI/CD pipeline. Let's take a look at three of the most popular CI/CD automation tools used in cloud environments: **Jenkins**, **CircleCI**, and **GitHub Actions**.

1. Jenkins

Jenkins is an open-source automation server widely used in CI/CD workflows. It provides plugins for building, deploying, and automating projects. Jenkins supports integration with a wide variety of third-party services and tools, including cloud services like AWS, Google Cloud, and Azure.

- **Features:**
    - **Pipeline as Code**: Jenkins supports defining pipelines using **Jenkinsfiles**, which are written in a domain-specific language (DSL).

    - **Extensibility**: Jenkins has a large plugin ecosystem, allowing teams to integrate it with numerous other tools, such as **Docker, Kubernetes, AWS**, and **Google Cloud**.

- Distributed Builds: Jenkins can distribute build
tasks across multiple machines, allowing for
scalable CI/CD operations.

- **Use Case**: Jenkins is ideal for organizations that need a
highly customizable and extensible CI/CD tool. It is
commonly used in both on-premises and cloud
environments for complex, multi-step automation pipelines.

2. CircleCI

CircleCI is a cloud-based CI/CD platform that provides a fast,
scalable, and customizable way to automate workflows. CircleCI
integrates seamlessly with **GitHub** and **Bitbucket** repositories, and
it provides support for Docker, Kubernetes, and cloud environments.

- **Features:**

  - **Docker Support**: CircleCI supports Docker natively,
    making it easy to containerize your application and
    manage dependencies.

  - **Parallelism**: CircleCI supports parallel builds,
    allowing you to run tests and deploy applications
    simultaneously, improving speed and efficiency.

  - **Cloud-Native**: CircleCI is fully cloud-based, meaning
    there's no need to manage infrastructure.

- **Use Case**: CircleCI is ideal for teams looking for a simple,
  fast, and scalable cloud-native CI/CD solution with a focus
  on containerized workflows.

3. GitHub Actions

GitHub Actions is GitHub's native CI/CD and automation tool, integrated directly into the GitHub ecosystem. It allows developers to automate workflows, including testing, building, and deploying applications, directly from their GitHub repositories.

- **Features**:

  - **Native GitHub Integration**: GitHub Actions integrates seamlessly with **GitHub repositories**, making it easy to trigger workflows on pull requests, commits, and other events.

  - **YAML-Based Configuration**: Workflows are defined in YAML files, making them easy to configure and version alongside the code.

  - **Flexibility**: GitHub Actions supports workflows for a wide range of applications, from simple build and test processes to complex, multi-step CI/CD pipelines.

- **Use Case**: GitHub Actions is ideal for developers already using GitHub as their source code repository. Its deep integration with GitHub and extensive documentation make it a great choice for teams that need simple, efficient automation for their CI/CD workflows.

Practical Project: Set Up a Simple CI/CD Pipeline on AWS, Google Cloud, or Azure

In this practical project, we will set up a simple CI/CD pipeline using **AWS CodePipeline**. This pipeline will automatically build, test, and deploy a sample application whenever code is committed to a Git repository. We will cover the essential steps involved in configuring a basic pipeline and demonstrate how you can integrate other services to enhance the pipeline's capabilities.

Step 1: Set Up the Code Repository

1. **Create a GitHub Repository**:

   o Create a new repository on **GitHub** and add a simple web application (e.g., a **Node.js** app or **Python Flask** app).

2. **Push the Code**:

   o Push the code to GitHub.

Step 2: Create AWS CodePipeline

1. **Navigate to AWS CodePipeline**:

   o Go to the **AWS CodePipeline** console and click "Create pipeline."

   o Define the pipeline name and select a new service role to allow CodePipeline to interact with other AWS services.

2. **Set Up Source Stage**:

- For the source stage, select **GitHub** as the source provider and authenticate your GitHub account.

- Choose the repository and branch that will trigger the pipeline whenever a new commit is made.

3. **Set Up Build Stage with CodeBuild:**

    - In the build stage, choose **AWS CodeBuild** as the build provider. Create a new build project.

    - In the build specification (buildspec.yml), define the build commands (e.g., npm install, npm run build, or pytest for Python).

4. **Set Up Deploy Stage with CodeDeploy or Elastic Beanstalk:**

    - For the deployment stage, choose **AWS Elastic Beanstalk** or **AWS CodeDeploy** as the deploy provider. Configure the environment (e.g., EC2 instance or Elastic Beanstalk environment).

Step 3: Test the Pipeline

1. **Push Code to GitHub:**

    - Make a change to the code (e.g., update the README or change a text value in the app) and push the changes to GitHub.

2. **Monitor the Pipeline:**

    - AWS CodePipeline will automatically trigger the build, test, and deployment process. You can monitor the pipeline's progress through the AWS Console.

Step 4: Verify Deployment

Once the pipeline completes, verify that the application is successfully deployed to your AWS environment (e.g., Elastic Beanstalk). You should be able to access the application through its public URL.

Conclusion

DevOps and continuous integration in the cloud are essential for modern software development, enabling faster development cycles, higher-quality software, and seamless deployment. Cloud providers like AWS, Google Cloud, and Azure offer powerful tools to automate CI/CD workflows, making it easier to manage the lifecycle of cloud applications. By implementing DevOps practices and CI/CD pipelines, developers can ensure that their applications are always in a deployable state, leading to faster releases and more reliable software. In this chapter, we've covered the fundamentals of DevOps, how to set up cloud-based CI/CD pipelines, and walked through a practical project to help you get hands-on experience with CI/CD automation in the cloud.

CHAPTER 12: CLOUD COST MANAGEMENT AND BILLING

Cloud computing has dramatically reshaped the way organizations build, scale, and deploy applications. One of the key advantages of the cloud is the ability to scale resources dynamically based on demand. However, with this flexibility comes the potential for significant cloud cost overruns if not properly managed. Understanding how cloud pricing works and having strategies in place to track, manage, and optimize costs is essential for any business looking to harness the full potential of cloud environments without sacrificing financial sustainability.

This chapter provides a deep dive into cloud pricing models, tools for managing cloud costs, and strategies to reduce unnecessary spending while maximizing the value of cloud services. We'll also walk you through a practical project where we calculate the cost of hosting a simple web application on AWS and discuss how to optimize configurations for cost savings.

Cloud Pricing Models

Cloud providers such as AWS, Google Cloud, and Azure offer various pricing models to accommodate different business needs and usage patterns. It's crucial to understand these pricing models because selecting the wrong model can lead to unforeseen costs or underutilized resources, ultimately impacting your budget.

1. Pay-as-You-Go

Pay-as-you-go (PAYG) is the most common cloud pricing model, where users pay only for the resources they actually use, without any upfront costs or long-term commitments. This model is extremely flexible and works well for businesses with fluctuating workloads or unpredictable usage patterns.

KEY FEATURES:

- **No Upfront Costs**: You only pay for what you consume, whether it's compute, storage, or bandwidth.

- **Elastic Scaling**: Resources can be dynamically scaled up or down depending on usage, meaning you're billed based on actual consumption.

- **Hourly or Per-Second Billing**: Many cloud services, like virtual machines (VMs) and compute instances, are billed by the hour or per second, depending on the provider.

Example: If you spin up a virtual machine on AWS, you are charged based on how long the VM is running. If you use 2 vCPUs and 8 GB of memory, the charge is based on the specific instance type and region for the time the instance is running. This model offers cost flexibility, but if resources are left running without being fully utilized, costs can add up quickly.

WHEN TO USE PAYG:

- **Unpredictable Workloads**: If your business has varying usage patterns or fluctuating traffic, the PAYG model is a good fit.

- **Testing and Development**: If you're running a test or development environment that doesn't need to be online all the time, PAYG allows you to pay only for what you use.

- **Startups or Small Businesses**: If you have limited upfront capital and need to scale gradually, PAYG allows you to avoid large upfront costs.

2. Reserved Instances

Reserved instances (RIs) are a cloud pricing model in which users commit to using a specific amount of cloud resources for a term (typically 1 to 3 years) in exchange for a discounted rate. This model is ideal for businesses with predictable usage patterns or applications that require steady and consistent resource consumption.

KEY FEATURES:

- **Upfront Commitment**: You commit to using a specific amount of resources for a set period (usually 1 to 3 years).

- **Cost Savings**: In return for the commitment, providers offer significant discounts—often up to 70%—compared to the pay-as-you-go model.

- **Varied Payment Options**: You can choose to pay for the entire reserved instance upfront, or opt for monthly payments over the term of the commitment.

Example: If you know that your application will need 2 EC2 instances with certain specifications running 24/7 for the next year, you can reserve those instances and receive a substantial discount. This is particularly beneficial for high-traffic applications, such as web servers, databases, and other services that need consistent, reliable performance.

WHEN TO USE RESERVED INSTANCES:

- **Predictable Workloads**: RIs are most effective for workloads that are predictable and will be running continuously over a long period.

- **High-Traffic Applications**: If you have an application that requires constant resources, such as a large e-commerce site or a data-intensive service, RIs can help you save costs.

- **Long-Term Projects**: If your project or service is expected to last over 1 to 3 years, reserved instances will help lock in savings.

3. Spot Instances

Spot instances (or **preemptible instances** in Google Cloud) are a cost-effective pricing model where users can bid on unused cloud capacity at significantly lower rates. However, the cloud provider can terminate these instances at any time if they need the capacity back.

KEY FEATURES:

- **Cost Savings**: Spot instances offer significant savings—up to 90%—compared to on-demand instances.

- **Preemptibility**: The cloud provider can terminate spot instances with little to no notice, typically within a 2-minute window, if the demand for resources increases.

- **Best for Fault-Tolerant Workloads**: Because of their volatility, spot instances are ideal for workloads that can tolerate interruptions, such as batch processing, large-scale data analytics, or background jobs.

Example: Suppose you need to run a large-scale data processing job, such as analyzing logs or generating reports, which can be stopped and resumed without major disruptions. Spot instances are perfect for these types of tasks, as you only pay a fraction of the cost compared to standard instances, but you must design your application to handle interruptions.

WHEN TO USE SPOT INSTANCES:

- **Non-Critical Workloads**: Spot instances are ideal for workloads that don't require guaranteed uptime or can tolerate interruptions, such as data processing, scientific simulations, and testing environments.

- **Batch Jobs**: Jobs that can be parallelized and don't rely on a fixed sequence of tasks can leverage spot instances for cost-effective scaling.

- **Flexible Projects**: Projects that can handle the termination of instances and can be restarted without significant overhead.

Managing Cloud Costs

Effectively managing cloud costs requires continuous monitoring, analysis, and optimization. Fortunately, cloud providers offer a variety of tools and services to track and reduce cloud expenses.

1. AWS Cost Explorer

AWS Cost Explorer is a tool that helps you visualize, analyze, and manage your AWS costs and usage. It provides interactive graphs that let you track your spending over time and gain insights into how resources are being utilized.

KEY FEATURES:

- **Cost and Usage Reports**: Visualize your AWS spending over time and analyze resource usage at a granular level.

- **Budgeting**: Set up budgets and get alerts when your costs exceed thresholds.

- **Cost Forecasting**: AWS Cost Explorer can predict future costs based on historical data, helping you plan and avoid unexpected expenses.

2. Google Cloud Billing and Cost Management Tools

Google Cloud provides **Billing Reports** and **Cost Management Tools** to help users track their cloud spending. The Google Cloud Console provides an easy-to-use dashboard that gives you insight into your spending patterns, and it can generate detailed billing reports for resource usage across different services.

KEY FEATURES:

- **Cost Breakdown**: Google Cloud's billing tools allow you to break down costs by project, region, or service, helping you identify areas of overspending.

- o **Budgets and Alerts**: You can set up budgets for specific projects or teams and get notifications if costs exceed predefined limits.

- o **Cost Forecasting**: Like AWS, Google Cloud provides predictive cost forecasts to help you plan your usage and avoid budget overruns.

3. Azure Cost Management + Billing

Azure Cost Management + Billing helps you track and manage your Azure costs and usage. With a user-friendly interface, it allows you to visualize spending patterns, set budgets, and make adjustments to optimize cloud resource consumption.

KEY FEATURES:

- o **Cost Analysis**: Azure provides detailed reports and visualizations to understand your cloud spending, including trends and spikes.

- o **Budgets**: Set custom budgets for specific departments, projects, or teams and receive notifications when you approach or exceed the limits.

- o **Recommendations**: Azure offers recommendations for optimizing your resources to reduce costs, such as resizing VMs or switching to more cost-effective pricing models.

4. Third-Party Tools

In addition to native cloud provider tools, there are several third-party cost management platforms that offer cross-cloud visibility and advanced optimization strategies, such as:

- **CloudHealth**: A popular cloud cost management platform that provides multi-cloud support, detailed reporting, and cost optimization recommendations.

- **CloudCheckr**: Offers deep cost analytics, governance, and security capabilities to optimize cloud usage and spending.

- **Spot by NetApp**: Focuses on providing automation for cost optimization using spot instances, auto-scaling, and workload management.

Cost-Effective Cloud Strategies: Best Practices for Saving Money in the Cloud

When using cloud computing, the key to saving money lies in how you manage and optimize your resources. Below are best practices for keeping cloud costs under control while maintaining high-performance applications.

1. Right-Sizing Instances

Ensure that the resources you provision match the actual requirements of your application. Over-provisioning leads to unnecessary costs, while under-provisioning can degrade performance.

- **Use Smaller Instances**: Start with smaller instances and scale up only if necessary. Many cloud providers offer a wide range of instance types to meet different workload needs.

- **Monitor Performance**: Regularly review your instance utilization using monitoring tools to identify underutilized resources that can be resized or terminated.

2. Leverage Auto-Scaling

Auto-scaling allows you to automatically adjust the number of instances based on traffic patterns. By scaling up during high demand and scaling down during low usage, you can avoid paying for idle resources.

- **Dynamic Scaling**: Set up auto-scaling policies that adjust your infrastructure based on performance metrics (e.g., CPU, memory, or network usage).

- **Use Cloud Functions**: Consider using serverless computing, such as **AWS Lambda** or **Google Cloud Functions**, where you pay only for the compute time used.

3. Use Reserved and Spot Instances

For predictable workloads, using reserved instances can provide significant savings. For workloads that can tolerate interruptions, spot instances offer substantial cost reductions.

- **Mix Reserved and On-Demand Instances**: Use reserved instances for steady, predictable workloads and spot instances for burst workloads that can be interrupted.

- **Avoid Over-Provisioning**: Reserve instances based on actual usage needs and not on the highest traffic levels.

4. Optimize Storage Costs

Data storage can become a significant cost if not properly managed. Consider these strategies to reduce storage costs:

- **Use Object Storage**: For infrequently accessed data, use lower-cost object storage solutions like **Amazon S3 Glacier**, **Google Coldline**, or **Azure Blob Storage**.

- **Data Tiering**: Store frequently accessed data in high-performance storage (e.g., **SSD** or **hot storage**) and move infrequently accessed data to cheaper, lower-performance storage options.

5. Clean Up Unused Resources

Ensure that you regularly review and delete unused resources, such as orphaned storage volumes, idle instances, and unneeded snapshots. Cloud providers often charge for resources that are not actively used, so it's essential to clean up resources to prevent waste.

Practical Project: Calculate the Cost of Hosting a Web App on AWS and Optimize the Configuration for Cost Savings

In this practical project, we'll walk through the process of calculating the cost of hosting a simple web application on **AWS**, and explore how to optimize the configuration for cost savings.

Step 1: Estimate Costs Using the AWS Pricing Calculator

1. **Create an AWS Account**: If you don't have one already, sign up for an AWS account at AWS.

2. **Use the AWS Pricing Calculator**: AWS provides a pricing calculator that helps estimate the cost of running a web app based on your resource requirements. Add resources such as **EC2 instances, RDS databases**, and **S3 storage** to the calculator to get an estimate of the monthly costs.

Step 2: Set Up EC2 Instance for Web App

1. **Launch an EC2 Instance**: Choose an EC2 instance type (e.g., **t3.micro**) based on your web app's requirements. Configure the instance with necessary settings such as security groups and key pairs.

2. **Install Web Server**: Install a web server (e.g., **Apache** or **Nginx**) on the instance and deploy your simple web application.

Step 3: Use Reserved Instances for Cost Savings

1. **Reserve EC2 Instances**: For predictable workloads, convert your EC2 instance to a reserved instance to take advantage of discounted rates.

2. **Apply Cost Calculations**: Update your AWS Pricing Calculator estimate to reflect the use of reserved instances instead of on-demand instances.

Step 4: Optimize Storage and Database Costs

1. **Use S3 for Static Files**: Offload static content (e.g., images, CSS, JS) to **Amazon S3**, which is cheaper than storing files on EC2.

2. **Use RDS with Reserved Instances**: If your application requires a database, set up **Amazon RDS** (e.g., MySQL or PostgreSQL) and reserve the instance for long-term savings.

Step 5: Test and Adjust

Monitor the actual usage and adjust the instance sizes, storage configurations, and databases to further optimize costs. Consider using auto-scaling to automatically adjust resources based on real-time demand.

Conclusion

Cloud cost management is a critical aspect of maintaining efficient, sustainable cloud infrastructure. By understanding cloud pricing models like **pay-as-you-go**, **reserved instances**, and **spot instances**, businesses can choose the right pricing strategy for their specific needs. Through the use of cloud cost management tools and best practices like right-sizing, auto-scaling, and cleaning up unused resources, companies can effectively optimize cloud costs. The practical project in this chapter provided hands-on experience in estimating cloud costs, setting up resources, and applying cost-saving strategies on AWS. By continuously monitoring usage and optimizing configurations, organizations can achieve cost-effective cloud computing while maintaining the performance and scalability they need.

CHAPTER 13: CLOUD COMPUTING FOR IOT (INTERNET OF THINGS)

The **Internet of Things (IoT)** is one of the most transformative technologies of the modern age, with its ability to connect billions of devices to the internet and enable seamless communication between them. Whether it's smart homes, wearable devices, industrial automation, or healthcare systems, IoT has revolutionized how devices and systems interact, share data, and respond in real-time. Central to the success of IoT is the integration with **cloud computing**, which provides the necessary infrastructure to handle the massive volume of data generated by IoT devices, process that data in real time, and store it for long-term analysis.

In this chapter, we will explore how IoT utilizes cloud computing for data collection, processing, and storage. We will take a close look at popular **IoT platforms** such as **AWS IoT**, **Azure IoT**, and **Google IoT Core**, and discuss their features and capabilities. Finally, we will guide you through a practical project where you will set up a basic IoT application to collect data from sensors and send it to the cloud for analysis. By the end of this chapter, you'll have a solid understanding of how IoT and cloud computing work together to create powerful, data-driven applications.

Connecting Devices to the Cloud: How IoT Uses Cloud for Data Collection, Processing, and Storage

The heart of IoT lies in the connection of various physical devices (sensors, actuators, or other embedded systems) to the internet. These devices generate large amounts of data—ranging from sensor readings like temperature, humidity, and motion, to more complex data like images or audio. Cloud computing is instrumental in managing and analyzing this data, providing the infrastructure needed to support these devices at scale.

1. Data Collection

Data collection is the first step in the IoT process. Devices, such as sensors, collect real-time data from their environment. These devices are typically designed with the capability to connect to the internet via wireless communication protocols like **Wi-Fi**, **Bluetooth**, **Zigbee**, **LoRaWAN**, and **5G**. Once data is collected, it needs to be transmitted to the cloud for further processing and storage.

- **Edge Devices and Gateways**: While IoT devices themselves may have the capability to collect data, many require an intermediary device known as an **IoT gateway** or **edge device**. These devices bridge the gap between local devices and the cloud, collecting, filtering, and preprocessing the data before sending it to the cloud for more intensive processing.

- **Connectivity**: Connectivity to the cloud is achieved through the internet or local network. Protocols such as **MQTT**, **HTTP**, and **CoAP** are commonly used to transmit data between IoT devices and cloud platforms, ensuring that data can be securely and efficiently transferred.

2. Data Processing

Once data is collected and transmitted to the cloud, the next step is data processing. **Cloud computing** enables the massive computational power needed to analyze data in real-time or batch processes. Data processing in the cloud involves:

- **Stream Processing**: Many IoT applications require real-time data processing (for example, monitoring the health of a machine in an industrial setting). This is where **stream processing** technologies, such as **AWS Kinesis**, **Google Cloud Dataflow**, or **Azure Stream Analytics**, come in. These services allow cloud platforms to process streams of incoming data from IoT devices instantaneously and make quick decisions based on that data.

- **Batch Processing**: For data that doesn't need to be processed immediately, batch processing can be used. This involves collecting large amounts of data over a period and then processing it in one go. Examples of batch processing tools include **AWS Lambda** for event-driven computing and **Google BigQuery** for big data analysis.

3. Data Storage

IoT devices generate huge volumes of data, and managing that data in a way that's accessible and scalable is one of the primary challenges of IoT systems. Cloud providers offer various storage options for IoT data, depending on the type and amount of data being generated.

- **Object Storage**: For unstructured data, such as logs or sensor data, cloud object storage is often used. **Amazon S3**, **Azure Blob Storage**, and **Google Cloud Storage** are popular services that allow for inexpensive, scalable storage solutions. These platforms can store vast amounts of data that can be accessed and analyzed at any time.

- **Time-Series Databases**: IoT data is often time-sensitive. For this reason, **time-series databases** are a common choice for storing sensor data. Services like **AWS Timestream**, **Azure Time Series Insights**, and **Google Cloud Bigtable** are designed to efficiently store and query time-series data generated by IoT devices.

- **Relational Databases**: For IoT systems that require structured data with relationships between entities (e.g., a smart home system storing user preferences alongside device information), traditional relational databases like **AWS RDS, Google Cloud SQL**, and **Azure SQL Database** can be used.

IoT Platforms: Overview of AWS IoT, Azure IoT, and Google IoT Core

Cloud IoT platforms play a crucial role in enabling the connection, management, and scaling of IoT devices and applications. These platforms offer a set of tools and services to connect IoT devices to the cloud, collect and analyze data, and manage devices. Let's explore three of the most prominent cloud IoT platforms: **AWS IoT**, **Azure IoT**, and **Google IoT Core**.

1. AWS IoT

AWS IoT is a comprehensive suite of services from Amazon Web Services that allows users to connect, manage, and analyze IoT devices at scale.

KEY FEATURES:

- **AWS IoT Core**: The central service for connecting IoT devices to the cloud. It supports secure device communication, data ingestion, and routing to various services for processing and storage.

- **Device Management**: AWS IoT offers tools to manage large fleets of devices, including automatic provisioning, over-the-air updates, and remote monitoring.

- **Analytics**: **AWS IoT Analytics** helps process, filter, and analyze data from IoT devices. It includes built-in integration with other AWS services such as **AWS Lambda** for custom processing, **Amazon S3** for storage, and **Amazon Kinesis** for real-time data streams.

- **Security**: AWS IoT provides robust security mechanisms, including end-to-end encryption, mutual authentication, and fine-grained access control through **AWS IoT Device Defender**.

2. Azure IoT

Azure IoT offers a set of services that enable users to build end-to-end IoT solutions with strong integration into Microsoft's ecosystem. It provides scalable solutions to connect, manage, and analyze IoT devices, as well as integrate IoT data into enterprise applications.

KEY FEATURES:

- **Azure IoT Hub**: The main service for connecting IoT devices to the Azure platform. IoT Hub supports secure communication, device management, and data processing.

- **Azure IoT Central**: A simplified, SaaS-based version of IoT Hub that allows users to quickly set up IoT solutions without deep technical expertise.

- **Azure Stream Analytics**: Real-time data analytics service that processes data from IoT devices and produces actionable insights in real time.

- **Azure Digital Twins**: A service for creating digital models of physical environments and devices, making it easy to simulate and monitor IoT ecosystems.

3. Google IoT Core

Google IoT Core is a fully managed service for securely connecting and managing IoT devices at scale. It provides real-time device data processing and integrates with Google Cloud's powerful machine learning and big data analytics tools.

KEY FEATURES:

- **Google Cloud IoT Core**: The central platform for managing IoT devices, offering secure device communication, data ingestion, and real-time monitoring.

- **Cloud Pub/Sub**: For asynchronous messaging, Cloud Pub/Sub helps in reliably transmitting data from IoT devices to Google Cloud for further processing.

- **Google Cloud Dataflow**: Real-time data processing service for transforming and analyzing streams of IoT data.

- **BigQuery**: Google's fully-managed, serverless data warehouse service allows users to analyze massive datasets from IoT devices in real time.

- **Google Cloud AI/ML**: Google Cloud provides a wide range of AI and machine learning tools that integrate with IoT data for predictive analysis and anomaly detection.

Practical Project: Set Up a Basic IoT Application that Collects Data from Sensors and Sends It to the Cloud for Analysis

In this practical project, we will walk through the process of setting up a simple IoT application using **AWS IoT Core**. We'll use a temperature and humidity sensor (e.g., **DHT11**) to collect data and send it to the cloud. Once the data is in the cloud, we will analyze it to detect any abnormal readings (e.g., if the temperature is too high).

Step 1: Set Up the IoT Device

1. **Choose a Sensor**: For this project, we will use a **DHT11** temperature and humidity sensor, which is widely used for basic IoT applications. The sensor connects to a microcontroller like **Raspberry Pi** or **Arduino**.

2. **Connect the Sensor to the Microcontroller**: Connect the **DHT11** sensor to the Raspberry Pi (or Arduino) via GPIO pins. Ensure that you have the necessary connections for power

(3.3V and GND) and data (the sensor's data pin to a GPIO pin on the Raspberry Pi).

3. **Install Required Libraries**: On your Raspberry Pi, install the necessary libraries to read data from the sensor. For example, for Raspberry Pi, you can use Python libraries like Adafruit_DHT to interface with the sensor.

bash

```
sudo pip install Adafruit_DHT
```

Step 2: Set Up AWS IoT Core

1. **Create an AWS Account**: If you don't already have one, sign up for an AWS account.

2. **Create an IoT Thing in AWS IoT Core**:

   o In the AWS Management Console, navigate to **AWS IoT Core** and create a new "Thing" to represent your IoT device.

   o Attach a policy to the Thing to allow it to publish data to AWS IoT Core.

3. **Generate and Download Device Certificates**: For secure communication between the sensor and the cloud, AWS IoT requires certificates. Download the device certificates and keep them safe, as you'll need them to connect your device securely.

4. **Set Up MQTT Client on the Raspberry Pi**: MQTT is the protocol used by AWS IoT Core for device communication. Install an MQTT client on your Raspberry Pi to send data.

bash

sudo pip install paho-mqtt

Step 3: Code the Device to Collect and Send Data

1. **Write the Code to Read Sensor Data:** Write a Python script to read the temperature and humidity data from the **DHT11** sensor.

python

```python
import Adafruit_DHT
import paho.mqtt.client as mqtt
import time

# Set sensor type and GPIO pin
sensor = Adafruit_DHT.DHT11
pin = 4

# MQTT setup
broker = 'your-iot-endpoint.amazonaws.com'
port = 8883
topic = 'iot/data'
client_id = 'sensor_device'

# Set up MQTT client
mqtt_client = mqtt.Client(client_id)
mqtt_client.tls_set('/path/to/root-CA.crt', '/path/to/certificate.pem.crt',
'/path/to/private.pem.key')
```

```
mqtt_client.connect(broker, port)

while True:
    # Read sensor data
    humidity, temperature = Adafruit_DHT.read_retry(sensor, pin)

    # Publish data to AWS IoT Core
    if humidity is not None and temperature is not None:
        payload = f'{{"temperature": {temperature}, "humidity": {humidity}}}'
        mqtt_client.publish(topic, payload)
        print(f'Sent data: {payload}')
    else:
        print('Failed to retrieve data from sensor')

    time.sleep(60)  # Collect data every 60 seconds
```

Step 4: Set Up Data Processing in the Cloud

1. **Create an IoT Rule**: In AWS IoT Core, create a rule that triggers when new data is received from your IoT device. This rule can store the data in an **S3 bucket**, trigger a **Lambda function** for further processing, or send the data to a **SQL database** like **AWS Timestream**.

2. **Analyze the Data**: Set up a **Lambda function** to process incoming IoT data. This function could check for anomalies, such as a temperature reading that exceeds a certain threshold.

Step 5: Monitor and Optimize

Monitor the IoT application in the AWS Management Console. Use **AWS CloudWatch** to view logs from your Lambda function and monitor the device's data flow.

Conclusion

Cloud computing plays a pivotal role in the success of the **Internet of Things (IoT)**, providing the infrastructure and scalability necessary to handle the vast amounts of data generated by connected devices. In this chapter, we've explored how IoT devices collect, process, and store data using cloud platforms like **AWS IoT**, **Azure IoT**, and **Google IoT Core**. We also walked through a practical project where we set up a basic IoT application that collects data from sensors, sends it to the cloud, and analyzes it.

With IoT and cloud computing, the possibilities are endless—from smart homes and cities to industrial automation and healthcare systems. By understanding how to connect devices to the cloud and optimize their performance, you can create IoT applications that are scalable, efficient, and cost-effective.

CHAPTER 14: FUTURE TRENDS IN CLOUD COMPUTING

Cloud computing is one of the most dynamic fields in technology, continuously evolving to meet the ever-growing demands of businesses, consumers, and developers. As we move into the next phase of digital transformation, several emerging trends are reshaping the landscape of cloud computing. These trends are driven by advancements in **artificial intelligence (AI), edge computing**, and **quantum computing**. Together, these technologies are not only enhancing the cloud's capabilities but are also paving the way for groundbreaking applications and services in industries like healthcare, finance, manufacturing, and beyond.

In this chapter, we will explore these future trends in-depth, starting with how **AI and machine learning (ML)** are being integrated into cloud platforms, followed by the rise of **edge computing** and its role in faster data processing. We will also take a closer look at the revolutionary field of **quantum computing** and its potential impact on the future of cloud technology. Finally, we will work through a practical project where you'll explore AI services from **AWS**, **Azure**, or **Google Cloud** to build a machine learning model.

Artificial Intelligence and Cloud: How AI and ML Are Integrated into Cloud Platforms

Artificial Intelligence (AI) and Machine Learning (ML) are no longer emerging technologies; they are here, and they are transforming the way businesses operate and make decisions. Cloud computing platforms have embraced AI and ML, offering powerful tools and services that enable businesses to harness these technologies without the need for specialized hardware or deep technical expertise. By leveraging the cloud's vast computing power, AI and ML models can be trained and deployed at scale, making them accessible to a broader range of industries.

1. AI and ML in Cloud Platforms

Cloud providers like **AWS**, **Google Cloud**, and **Azure** have integrated AI and ML into their ecosystems, offering a range of pre-built and customizable tools for developers, data scientists, and business analysts.

- **AWS AI and ML Services**: AWS offers a comprehensive suite of AI and ML tools, including **Amazon SageMaker**, which enables developers to build, train, and deploy machine learning models quickly and efficiently. AWS also provides AI services like **Amazon Polly** (text-to-speech), **Amazon Rekognition** (image and video analysis), and **Amazon Lex** (chatbots).

- **Google Cloud AI and ML Services**: Google Cloud provides services like **AI Platform** for building custom machine learning models, and **BigQuery ML** for running ML models directly on BigQuery without needing deep expertise in ML. Google also offers advanced AI tools like **AutoML**, which allows users to train custom models with little to no machine learning experience.

- **Azure AI and ML Services**: Azure has embraced AI with services like **Azure Machine Learning**, a cloud-based service that provides everything from data preparation to model training and deployment. Azure also offers pre-built AI solutions like **Azure Cognitive Services** for language, vision, and speech processing.

2. How AI and ML Are Transforming Business Operations

AI and ML are fundamentally changing the way organizations operate by automating complex tasks, improving decision-making, and providing personalized customer experiences. Here's a breakdown of how these technologies are applied in the cloud:

- **Data Processing and Analytics**: Cloud-based AI services can process vast amounts of data quickly and accurately. For example, financial institutions use AI to analyze market trends, detect fraudulent activities, and make investment decisions. Healthcare providers leverage AI to analyze medical images and predict patient outcomes.

- **Natural Language Processing (NLP)**: AI-powered NLP tools, available in the cloud, are being used for customer service (e.g., chatbots) and document analysis. For instance, **AWS Comprehend** or **Azure Cognitive Services** help businesses automate sentiment analysis and text summarization, reducing manual labor and improving customer insights.

- **Automation and Robotics**: AI integrated into cloud platforms allows for the automation of repetitive tasks.

Robotics in manufacturing, for example, uses AI to optimize production lines, predict maintenance needs, and improve operational efficiency.

- **AI-Powered Personalization**: Retailers are using cloud-based AI services to analyze customer behavior, preferences, and browsing history to provide personalized shopping experiences. This leads to improved customer engagement and higher sales.

3. The Benefits of Cloud-Enabled AI and ML

- **Scalability**: Cloud platforms provide virtually unlimited computational power, which is crucial for training complex AI models. This means businesses can scale their AI and ML projects without worrying about hardware limitations.

- **Cost Efficiency**: Instead of investing in costly on-premise hardware and infrastructure, organizations can use cloud-based AI and ML tools on a pay-as-you-go basis, reducing upfront costs and operational expenses.

- **Accessibility**: Cloud-based AI services are designed to be user-friendly, allowing individuals without deep machine learning expertise to integrate AI into their applications. With pre-built models and APIs, even small businesses can leverage the power of AI.

Edge Computing: The Role of Edge Computing in Cloud Networks for Faster Data Processing

Edge computing refers to the practice of processing data closer to where it is generated (at the "edge" of the network), rather than sending it to a centralized cloud data center for processing. This approach reduces latency, conserves bandwidth, and enables real-time decision-making, which is particularly important for applications like IoT, autonomous vehicles, and augmented reality.

1. How Edge Computing Works

In traditional cloud computing, data generated by devices is transmitted to data centers for processing. However, this method can introduce significant latency, especially when dealing with real-time applications. **Edge computing** addresses this problem by moving data processing to local devices, edge servers, or micro data centers closer to the point of data collection.

- **Edge Devices**: These are local devices or sensors that generate data, such as smart cameras, industrial machinery, or autonomous vehicles. The edge device either processes the data locally or forwards it to an edge server.

- **Edge Servers**: These servers are positioned closer to the source of data collection, often within a local network or in geographically distributed locations. Edge servers process data locally and may communicate with the cloud for deeper analysis if necessary.

- **Cloud Integration**: While edge computing minimizes the need for round-trip communication to the cloud, it does not replace the cloud. The cloud serves as a central hub for long-term storage, analysis, and sharing of data, while the edge focuses on real-time processing and low-latency applications.

2. The Benefits of Edge Computing in Cloud Networks

- **Reduced Latency**: By processing data at the edge, devices can respond much faster than if data had to be sent to a distant data center for processing. This is crucial for time-sensitive applications like autonomous vehicles or real-time video streaming.

- **Bandwidth Efficiency**: Sending large amounts of data to the cloud for processing can strain bandwidth. By processing data locally, edge computing reduces the amount of data that needs to be transmitted, leading to more efficient use of network resources.

- **Real-Time Decision Making**: Edge computing enables devices to make decisions without relying on the cloud. For example, in industrial IoT applications, machines can detect issues in real time and trigger corrective actions immediately, without needing cloud-based intervention.

- **Scalability**: Edge computing allows for the processing of data from thousands or millions of devices locally, ensuring that the cloud isn't overwhelmed with excessive data. As IoT continues to grow, edge computing will become increasingly critical in managing and scaling IoT infrastructures.

3. Real-World Use Cases for Edge Computing

- **Autonomous Vehicles**: Autonomous vehicles generate large amounts of data from sensors and cameras. Edge computing processes this data locally to enable quick decision-making, such as stopping for obstacles or adjusting speed based on road conditions, without waiting for cloud-based analysis.

- **Smart Cities**: Edge computing is used in smart cities to process data from sensors like traffic cameras, environmental sensors, and smart meters. Local processing ensures quick responses, such as controlling traffic lights, managing waste collection, and monitoring pollution levels.

- **Healthcare**: In remote healthcare applications, edge computing allows medical devices (like heart monitors or infusion pumps) to process patient data locally, enabling faster responses and reducing the need for constant cloud connectivity.

- **Manufacturing**: Industrial IoT applications use edge computing to monitor production lines in real-time, detect anomalies, and perform predictive maintenance on machinery, improving efficiency and reducing downtime.

4. Cloud-Edge Integration

While edge computing offers numerous benefits, it still relies on the cloud for long-term storage, advanced analytics, and machine learning. The **cloud-edge hybrid model** enables organizations to leverage the best of both worlds: local processing at the edge for real-time responses and centralized cloud computing for advanced analysis and data storage.

Quantum Computing: A Brief Introduction to Quantum Computing's Role in the Future of Cloud

Quantum computing is a rapidly advancing field that promises to revolutionize computing by using quantum-mechanical phenomena, such as **superposition** and **entanglement**, to perform computations that are impossible for classical computers to achieve in a reasonable time. While still in its infancy, quantum computing has the potential to impact cloud computing by enabling faster problem-solving for complex applications in fields like cryptography, materials science, and optimization.

1. What is Quantum Computing?

Quantum computers differ from classical computers in that they use **quantum bits** (qubits) instead of binary bits. While classical computers use 0s and 1s, qubits can represent both 0 and 1 simultaneously due to **superposition**, allowing quantum computers to explore many possible solutions in parallel. Additionally, qubits can be **entangled**, meaning the state of one qubit can directly influence the state of another, even across large distances.

These properties allow quantum computers to perform certain types of calculations exponentially faster than classical computers, making them particularly suited for tasks like factoring large numbers, simulating quantum systems, or solving complex optimization problems.

2. The Role of Quantum Computing in Cloud

Cloud providers have already started experimenting with quantum computing by offering **quantum computing as a service**. These services allow developers to access quantum processors remotely and experiment with quantum algorithms without needing to own specialized hardware.

- **AWS Braket**: AWS offers **Amazon Braket**, a fully managed service that provides access to quantum computing hardware from various providers like **D-Wave, IonQ**, and **Rigetti**. Amazon Braket enables users to explore quantum algorithms and run simulations in the cloud.

- **Azure Quantum**: Microsoft's **Azure Quantum** is another quantum computing service that provides access to both quantum simulators and quantum hardware. Azure Quantum supports several quantum hardware providers and is designed to be integrated into existing Azure services.

- **Google Quantum AI**: Google offers **Quantum AI**, which provides quantum computing hardware and software tools for developers. Google's **Quantum Engine** is a cloud-based platform for quantum computation that allows users to run quantum algorithms.

3. Future Potential of Quantum Cloud Computing

Although quantum computers are not yet capable of replacing classical computers for most everyday tasks, they are expected to play a crucial role in specific fields:

- **Cryptography**: Quantum computers could break existing encryption schemes, such as RSA and ECC, by efficiently factoring large numbers. This has led to research into **post-**

quantum cryptography to create encryption algorithms that are resistant to quantum attacks.

- **Material Science and Drug Discovery**: Quantum computers can simulate molecular structures and chemical reactions with high precision, which could revolutionize material science and drug discovery by enabling researchers to quickly find new compounds and materials.

- **Optimization Problems**: Quantum computers excel at solving complex optimization problems that involve many variables, such as supply chain management, route optimization, and financial portfolio management.

Practical Project: Explore AI Services from AWS, Azure, or GCP to Build a Machine Learning Model

In this practical project, we will build a machine learning model using AI services from **AWS**, **Azure**, or **Google Cloud**. We'll focus on using **AWS SageMaker, Azure Machine Learning**, or **Google AI Platform** to train a model that predicts housing prices based on features such as location, size, and number of rooms.

Step 1: Set Up the Cloud Environment

1. **Create an Account**: Sign up for an account with **AWS, Azure**, or **Google Cloud**.

2. **Create a Project**: For this project, create a new machine learning project in the cloud console. Select the **SageMaker, Azure ML**, or **Google AI Platform** service to get started.

Step 2: Data Preparation

1. **Dataset**: Download a publicly available dataset, such as the **Boston Housing Dataset**, which contains features like square footage, number of rooms, and location, along with the target variable (housing price).

2. **Preprocessing**: Use the platform's built-in tools to clean and preprocess the data, handling missing values and normalizing the data.

Step 3: Build the Model

1. **Choose an Algorithm**: Select a machine learning algorithm, such as **Linear Regression**, that is suitable for predicting continuous values (e.g., housing prices).

2. **Train the Model**: Use the platform's UI or APIs to train the model on the prepared data. The platform will automatically split the data into training and validation sets and run the training process.

Step 4: Evaluate the Model

1. **Performance Metrics**: Evaluate the model's performance using common regression metrics such as **mean absolute error (MAE), mean squared error (MSE)**, and **R-squared**.

2. **Optimization**: If the model's performance is suboptimal, you can adjust hyperparameters, choose a different algorithm, or collect more data to improve predictions.

3.

Step 5: Deploy the Model

1. **Deployment**: Once satisfied with the model's performance, deploy it to the cloud for making real-time predictions via a REST API endpoint. AWS SageMaker, Azure ML, and Google AI Platform all offer easy deployment options.

Conclusion

The future of cloud computing is closely intertwined with cutting-edge technologies like **AI**, **edge computing**, and **quantum computing**. As cloud platforms continue to evolve, they are empowering businesses to leverage these technologies at scale, providing them with unprecedented computational power and flexibility. In this chapter, we've explored how AI and ML are integrated into cloud platforms, the importance of edge computing for real-time processing, and the revolutionary potential of quantum computing. Through the practical project, you also gained hands-on experience with cloud-based AI services, setting you up to harness the power of these emerging technologies in your own applications. As we look ahead, the possibilities for cloud computing continue to expand, making it an exciting time for developers, businesses, and consumers alike.

CHAPTER 15: WRAPPING UP: CONTINUING YOUR CLOUD JOURNEY

As we reach the conclusion of this journey through cloud computing, it's essential to reflect on the knowledge you've gained and look ahead to the future. The cloud is an ever-evolving landscape, and the skills you've developed here are just the beginning of your journey into one of the most exciting and transformative fields in technology. In this chapter, we will outline the next steps for continuing your cloud learning, building a career in cloud computing, and staying up-to-date with the fast-paced changes in the cloud industry. Additionally, we'll guide you through a final practical project where you will build and deploy a multi-component application using a combination of **IaaS**, **PaaS**, and **SaaS** services.

Next Steps: What to Learn Next— Exploring Advanced Cloud Services, Certifications, and Real-World Case Studies

The cloud computing space is vast, and now that you've developed a foundational understanding, it's time to dive deeper. To truly master cloud technologies, you'll need to explore more advanced topics and specialize in areas that align with your career goals or project needs.

1. Advanced Cloud Services

After mastering the basics of cloud computing, the next step is to explore advanced cloud services offered by major cloud providers like AWS, Azure, and Google Cloud. These services enable more sophisticated workflows, large-scale deployments, and enterprise-level applications.

- **AWS Advanced Services:**

    o **Amazon Elastic Kubernetes Service (EKS)**: Learn container orchestration using Kubernetes and deploy containerized applications at scale.

    o **AWS Lambda and Serverless**: Explore serverless computing, where you run code in response to events without provisioning or managing servers.

    o **Amazon SageMaker**: Dive into machine learning on the cloud with SageMaker, allowing you to build, train, and deploy machine learning models.

- **Azure Advanced Services:**

    o **Azure Kubernetes Service (AKS)**: Learn how to manage containerized applications using Kubernetes on Azure.

    o **Azure Functions**: Master serverless computing in the Azure ecosystem, building lightweight applications that scale automatically.

- o **Azure AI and Cognitive Services**: Expand into AI and machine learning, learning how to integrate intelligent applications into cloud solutions.

- **Google Cloud Advanced Services**:

  - o **Google Kubernetes Engine (GKE)**: Delve into Google's managed Kubernetes service for automating deployment, scaling, and operations of containerized applications.

  - o **Google BigQuery**: Explore Google's serverless, highly scalable, and cost-effective multi-cloud data warehouse for big data analytics.

  - o **Google Cloud AI Platform**: Build advanced AI and ML models using Google's machine learning services, which integrate with TensorFlow and other AI technologies.

By gaining proficiency in these advanced services, you will be equipped to handle complex cloud infrastructure and cutting-edge use cases, such as machine learning models, containerized applications, and data processing at scale.

2. Cloud Certifications

Cloud certifications are a great way to validate your skills and enhance your credibility in the cloud computing space. Obtaining certifications not only proves your expertise but also opens doors to advanced roles and higher-paying jobs in cloud technology.

- **AWS Certifications**:

- **AWS Certified Solutions Architect – Associate**: Ideal for those looking to build expertise in designing scalable and cost-effective cloud architectures.

- **AWS Certified DevOps Engineer**: This certification focuses on continuous delivery, automation, and scaling in the AWS environment.

- **AWS Certified Machine Learning – Specialty**: Perfect for those interested in machine learning and AI in the AWS cloud.

- **Microsoft Azure Certifications**:

  - **Microsoft Certified: Azure Solutions Architect Expert**: Aimed at professionals designing and implementing solutions on Azure.

  - **Microsoft Certified: Azure DevOps Engineer Expert**: For those working with Azure DevOps to automate, scale, and deploy cloud environments.

  - **Microsoft Certified: Azure AI Engineer Associate**: A certification designed for professionals working with AI solutions and machine learning on Azure.

- **Google Cloud Certifications**:

  - **Google Cloud Certified – Professional Cloud Architect**: This certification validates your ability to design, develop, and manage cloud solutions on Google Cloud.

  - **Google Cloud Certified – Associate Cloud Engineer**: Focused on implementing and managing Google Cloud resources.

- Google Cloud Certified – Professional Data Engineer: This is ideal for those interested in big data and machine learning services on Google Cloud.

Taking these certifications will solidify your understanding of cloud computing concepts and ensure you are well-versed in best practices and cloud provider-specific tools.

3. Real-World Case Studies

Learning through real-world examples is a powerful way to deepen your understanding of cloud computing. Analyzing how companies leverage cloud technologies to solve business problems gives you practical insights into cloud infrastructure.

- **Netflix on AWS**: Learn how Netflix uses AWS for its global streaming platform, handling millions of concurrent users while leveraging tools like **Amazon S3, AWS Lambda**, and **Amazon DynamoDB**.

- **Uber on Google Cloud**: Explore how Uber uses Google Cloud's **BigQuery, Google Kubernetes Engine**, and **Cloud Spanner** to process massive amounts of ride data in real-time and maintain high availability.

- **Microsoft Azure in the Enterprise**: Examine how enterprises use Azure to create hybrid cloud solutions and leverage **Azure Active Directory, Azure Machine Learning**, and **Azure Kubernetes Service** to modernize their IT infrastructure.

By studying these case studies, you will gain practical insights into how large organizations use cloud technologies and how you can replicate these architectures for your own projects.

Building a Career in Cloud Computing: Resources and Tips for Breaking into Cloud Computing as a Career

Cloud computing is one of the fastest-growing fields in the tech industry, with increasing demand for cloud professionals in areas like architecture, DevOps, data science, security, and more. Whether you're just starting out or transitioning from another IT field, here are some tips to help you break into cloud computing:

1. Learn the Fundamentals

Before diving into more advanced topics, it's important to have a solid understanding of cloud computing basics. Review the core concepts of **IaaS**, **PaaS**, **SaaS**, cloud storage, and cloud networking. Familiarize yourself with the major cloud providers—AWS, Azure, and Google Cloud—and their respective services.

2. Build Hands-On Experience

The best way to learn cloud computing is by doing. Set up your own projects in the cloud, such as hosting a website, building a simple database, or deploying a basic application. Many cloud providers offer free-tier services, which allow you to experiment without incurring costs.

- **AWS Free Tier**: AWS offers a free tier that includes services like EC2, S3, and DynamoDB, allowing you to gain hands-on experience with minimal investment.

- **Azure Free Account**: Azure offers a free account with access to a range of services, including **Azure Virtual Machines**, **Azure Blob Storage**, and **Azure SQL Database**.

- **Google Cloud Free Tier**: Google Cloud provides a free tier with access to services like **Google Compute Engine**, **Google Cloud Functions**, and **Google Cloud Storage**.

3. Join Cloud Communities

Cloud computing has a vibrant and active community. Engaging with the community can provide you with valuable resources, industry insights, and networking opportunities.

- **AWS re:Invent**: The annual AWS re:Invent conference is a great opportunity to learn about the latest AWS products and services, attend technical sessions, and meet industry professionals.

- **Azure Meetups**: Join local or virtual Azure meetups to network with professionals and learn about the latest developments in Azure technologies.

- **Cloud Computing Forums**: Participate in online communities like Stack Overflow, Reddit, and LinkedIn groups to connect with other cloud professionals and seek advice on cloud-related topics.

4. Keep Learning

The cloud computing landscape evolves rapidly, so staying up-to-date with the latest trends, services, and best practices is essential. Subscribe to cloud-related blogs, follow industry leaders on social media, and attend webinars or conferences to keep learning and expanding your knowledge.

Staying Updated with Cloud Technologies: How to Keep Learning and Stay Up-to-Date with the Ever-Evolving Cloud Landscape

Cloud technologies are advancing at an incredible pace. To remain relevant in the field, it's essential to keep up with new developments, emerging technologies, and best practices. Here's how you can stay updated:

1. Follow Key Cloud Providers' Updates

- **AWS News Blog**: AWS frequently updates its blog with announcements about new services, features, and tutorials. Stay informed by following this blog to understand the latest AWS innovations.

- **Azure Blog**: Microsoft's Azure blog is a great resource for updates on Azure's features, capabilities, and integration with other Microsoft technologies.

- **Google Cloud Blog**: Google Cloud's blog offers insights into the company's latest cloud solutions, case studies, and real-time updates on the evolving landscape of cloud services.

2. Enroll in Cloud Courses and Certifications

Cloud certifications are not just valuable for job opportunities—they are also an excellent way to stay updated on the latest cloud technologies. Consider enrolling in cloud courses to deepen your expertise:

- **AWS Training and Certification**: AWS offers a range of training resources, including online courses, webinars, and hands-on labs.

- **Microsoft Learn**: Microsoft Learn provides free, self-paced learning paths for Azure, covering everything from beginner to advanced topics.

- **Google Cloud Training**: Google Cloud offers various training programs and certification exams to help you master Google Cloud technologies.

3. Read Books and Watch Webinars

Books and webinars are excellent ways to stay up-to-date with cloud technologies. Many cloud experts publish books that go deep into specific cloud topics or new services. Webinars and online events hosted by cloud providers or independent platforms provide a platform to interact with cloud professionals and learn about new tools and strategies.

- **Cloud Academy** and **A Cloud Guru**: These platforms offer both books and webinars to help you stay ahead of the curve in cloud computing.

- **AWS Online Training**: AWS frequently hosts webinars on specific services or solutions, which can be incredibly useful for staying updated on new offerings.

4. Experiment with Emerging Cloud Trends

As the cloud evolves, new technologies like **edge computing**, **quantum computing**, and **serverless architectures** are reshaping the way businesses use the cloud. Stay updated by experimenting with these technologies and integrating them into your projects.

Final Practical Project: Build and Deploy a Multi-Component Application Using IaaS, PaaS, and SaaS Services

In this final practical project, we'll apply what we've learned to build a multi-component cloud application using a combination of **IaaS**, **PaaS**, and **SaaS** services. We'll create a simple web application with a frontend, backend, and database, and deploy it to a cloud provider.

Step 1: Set Up the Frontend (IaaS)

1. **Create an EC2 Instance (AWS)** or **VM (Azure/Google Cloud)** to host the frontend. Choose an appropriate instance type for a lightweight web application (e.g., t2.micro on AWS).

2. **Install a Web Server**: Install **Apache** or **Nginx** on the instance to serve your frontend application.

3. **Upload Frontend Code**: Upload your HTML, CSS, and JavaScript files to the server and configure the web server to serve the application.

Step 2: Set Up the Backend (PaaS)

1. **Create a PaaS Application**: Use **AWS Elastic Beanstalk**, **Azure App Service**, or **Google App Engine** to create a backend service (e.g., Node.js, Python Flask).

2. **Deploy Backend Code**: Push your backend code to the cloud service using the built-in deployment tools. Configure the service to interact with your database and handle requests from the frontend.

Step 3: Set Up the Database (SaaS)

1. **Choose a Database Service**: Use a managed database service like **Amazon RDS**, **Azure SQL Database**, or **Google Cloud SQL** for the backend database.

2. **Create Database Schema**: Define the schema for storing user data, application settings, etc.

3. **Connect Backend to Database**: Ensure that the backend is connected to the database to read/write data as needed.

Step 4: Test and Deploy

Once the application is deployed, test its functionality by navigating to the frontend and verifying that the backend and database are working as expected. Ensure proper security settings and performance optimizations are in place before launching the application publicly.

Conclusion

The cloud computing journey is an ongoing one. In this chapter, we've outlined the key next steps for continuing your education in the field, whether through exploring advanced cloud services, obtaining certifications, or analyzing real-world case studies. We've also discussed how to build a career in cloud computing and the importance of staying up-to-date with emerging technologies. Finally, the practical project provided hands-on experience with building and deploying a multi-component cloud application using a combination of IaaS, PaaS, and SaaS services.

As cloud technologies continue to evolve, there will always be new opportunities to learn, innovate, and grow. Embrace the future of cloud computing by continuing to build on the foundation you've established here. The possibilities are limitless.

CONCLUSION: EMPOWERING YOU TO BUILD WITH THE CLOUD

As we reach the end of this journey through the world of cloud computing, it's important to take a step back and reflect on the incredible progress you've made. By now, you have built a solid foundation in cloud computing technologies, understanding both the concepts and practical applications that make the cloud an indispensable tool in modern software development and business operations. From virtual machines and serverless computing to machine learning and edge computing, you've not only explored key cloud services but also acquired the technical skills to work with these services in real-world projects.

Now, as you stand at the threshold of your cloud journey, it's time to look ahead. This final section is about empowering you to tackle your next cloud computing project with confidence. You've learned the basics, explored advanced topics, and had hands-on experience with tools and services across multiple cloud platforms. It's time to take those skills and apply them to solve real-world problems, build scalable applications, and continue your path towards cloud mastery.

Let's recap the key concepts you've learned in this book, and set the stage for the exciting cloud projects and career opportunities that lie ahead.

Recap of Key Concepts Learned

In this book, we've covered a vast range of cloud computing concepts, tools, and services across major cloud platforms such as AWS, Microsoft Azure, and Google Cloud. Here's a look back at the most important takeaways:

1. Core Cloud Computing Models

You began by understanding the fundamental cloud models: **IaaS**, **PaaS**, and **SaaS**. These models form the backbone of cloud computing, each serving a unique purpose in the ecosystem:

- **IaaS** (Infrastructure as a Service) provides you with the foundational infrastructure components like virtual machines, storage, and networks. With IaaS, you manage the software stack on top of the infrastructure, giving you flexibility in configuring your environment.

- **PaaS** (Platform as a Service) simplifies the development process by providing a fully managed environment where developers can focus on building and deploying applications without worrying about managing infrastructure or runtime environments.

- **SaaS** (Software as a Service) delivers software applications via the cloud, where you pay for the usage of the app rather than managing or maintaining it yourself.

These models together allow businesses and developers to choose the right combination of infrastructure, platform, and software services based on their specific needs, budget, and scalability requirements.

2. Cloud Storage and Data Management

Another key concept was cloud storage, which is crucial for handling massive amounts of data in cloud computing environments. You explored how cloud platforms provide scalable, secure, and cost-effective storage solutions:

- **Object Storage** (Amazon S3, Google Cloud Storage, Azure Blob Storage) is ideal for unstructured data like documents, images, and backups.

- **Block Storage** is used for applications requiring frequent updates and low-latency access to data.

- **File Storage** solutions offer network-attached storage for shared files and enterprise use cases.

You also learned about **data processing** tools like **AWS Lambda** for serverless computing, where you can run your code in response to specific events without needing to manage servers.

3. Cloud Networking and Content Delivery

Cloud networking and content delivery are critical components of any cloud-based application. You explored how cloud services allow users to connect resources securely, efficiently, and with minimal latency:

- **Virtual Private Cloud (VPC)** allows you to create isolated environments within the cloud, securing communication between cloud resources.

- **Content Delivery Networks (CDNs)** improve the speed of content delivery to end users, ensuring fast and responsive applications, regardless of geographic location.

By mastering these concepts, you're now equipped to design scalable, high-performance, and secure applications that can operate globally.

4. Security in the Cloud

With the increased adoption of cloud services comes the responsibility to secure your data and applications. You learned how to approach cloud security, understanding the importance of:

- **Identity and Access Management (IAM)** for controlling who can access your resources.

- **Encryption** for protecting sensitive data both at rest and in transit.

- **Compliance and Governance** for ensuring your cloud deployments meet industry standards and legal requirements.

Securing cloud-based applications is paramount, and having the skills to implement robust security measures is crucial for any cloud engineer or developer.

5. DevOps and Continuous Integration/Continuous Delivery (CI/CD)

You also explored the transformative power of **DevOps** and **CI/CD** in cloud computing. DevOps is the practice of integrating development and operations to streamline software delivery and infrastructure management. With CI/CD pipelines, you learned how to:

- Automate code integration and testing to ensure that new features are delivered quickly and without introducing errors.

- Deploy applications seamlessly using cloud-based tools like **AWS CodePipeline, Azure DevOps**, or **Google Cloud Build**.

- Monitor and optimize cloud applications for performance and cost.

The integration of **automation** in the DevOps lifecycle is key to improving speed, reducing manual work, and ensuring that your cloud-based applications are always production-ready.

6. Advanced Cloud Services: AI, Edge Computing, and Quantum Computing

In the later chapters, we explored some of the most exciting trends in cloud computing:

- **Artificial Intelligence (AI)** and **Machine Learning (ML)** are transforming industries by making cloud-based services more intelligent and adaptive. You explored cloud services like **AWS SageMaker, Azure Machine Learning**, and **Google AI Platform** to build AI-driven applications.

- **Edge Computing** allows for faster data processing by moving computation closer to the data source. This reduces latency and is critical for IoT devices, autonomous vehicles, and other time-sensitive applications.

- **Quantum Computing** is on the horizon and promises to solve complex computational problems that classical computers cannot handle, such as optimization problems, cryptography, and simulations.

These emerging technologies have the potential to revolutionize the way cloud computing is used, and staying abreast of these developments will position you at the forefront of the industry.

7. Real-World Cloud Applications and Case Studies

Throughout the book, you examined how major companies leverage cloud computing to solve real-world problems. From **Netflix** using AWS to deliver content to millions of users, to **Uber** leveraging Google Cloud for ride data processing, these case studies provided practical insights into how cloud technologies are used at scale. By learning from these examples, you now have a deeper understanding of how to architect, deploy, and manage cloud-based solutions that can handle large amounts of traffic, data, and complexity.

Motivating You to Tackle Your Next Cloud Computing Project with Confidence

As you look ahead to the next steps in your cloud computing journey, it's important to remember that cloud computing is a dynamic and ever-evolving field. It is impossible to master every tool or service right away, but with the foundation you've built in this book, you are now well-equipped to tackle a wide range of cloud-based challenges.

Here's how you can approach your next project with confidence:

1. Start Small, Think Big

When starting a new cloud project, it's important to start small and progressively build on your knowledge. Start with a simple application, such as a basic website, blog, or small-scale backend service. As you grow more comfortable with the cloud platform you're working on, you can scale your project to incorporate more advanced features, such as integrating machine learning models, implementing serverless architecture, or using container orchestration.

The key is not to try and do everything at once but to break the project into manageable tasks and add complexity incrementally.

2. Embrace Cloud-Native Solutions

Cloud-native architecture is designed to take full advantage of cloud computing capabilities, enabling scalable, resilient, and cost-effective applications. Leverage services like **AWS Lambda** (serverless), **Google Kubernetes Engine** (container orchestration), or **Azure Functions** (event-driven compute) to design cloud-native solutions that are flexible and scalable from the outset.

By embracing the cloud-native approach, you are ensuring that your applications are optimized for the cloud and can scale efficiently as usage grows.

3. Collaborate and Learn from the Cloud Community

Cloud computing is a community-driven field, and there are abundant resources and people willing to help you succeed. Join cloud forums, participate in meetups, and follow cloud professionals on platforms like LinkedIn or Twitter. Engaging with others who have real-world experience can help you solve problems more quickly and keep you motivated as you work through challenges.

The cloud community is an excellent source of advice, and it's important to continuously learn from others who may have encountered similar challenges or have tips and tricks to share.

4. Continuously Update Your Skills

The cloud is constantly evolving, with new services, tools, and best practices emerging every day. To stay relevant in this field, it's crucial to keep learning. Follow the blogs, attend webinars, and take courses related to cloud computing. Services like **AWS Training**, **Google Cloud Learning**, and **Microsoft Learn** offer free and paid resources to help you stay on top of new cloud technologies and trends.

Additionally, pursuing cloud certifications like the **AWS Certified Solutions Architect**, **Google Professional Cloud Architect**, or **Microsoft Certified: Azure Solutions Architect** can help you gain in-depth knowledge of specific cloud platforms and validate your skills for career advancement.

5. Focus on Real-World Applications

One of the best ways to solidify your knowledge and boost your confidence is by building real-world applications. Whether you're building a portfolio website, deploying a small e-commerce store, or creating a data pipeline for analytics, the experience you gain from working on real-world projects will be invaluable.

The knowledge you've gained here has given you the foundation, but real-world applications are where you'll learn to solve complex problems and deal with the intricacies of cloud computing.

Final Practical Project: Build and Deploy a Multi-Component Application Using IaaS, PaaS, and SaaS Services

In this final project, you will put everything you've learned into practice by building and deploying a multi-component application using a combination of **IaaS**, **PaaS**, and **SaaS** services. Here's an overview of the steps you'll take to complete the project:

Step 1: Set Up the IaaS Environment

1. **Provision Virtual Machines (VMs)**: Set up the compute resources using an IaaS service, such as **AWS EC2, Azure Virtual Machines,** or **Google Compute Engine.** These VMs will serve as the backend infrastructure for your application.

2. **Configure Networking**: Set up a Virtual Private Cloud (VPC) to create a secure and isolated network for your application. Configure the necessary security groups, subnets, and routing tables to ensure that your application is properly secured.

Step 2: Set Up the PaaS Environment

1. **Deploy the Application on PaaS**: Use a **PaaS** service such as **AWS Elastic Beanstalk, Azure App Services,** or **Google App Engine** to deploy the frontend and backend of your application. This service will handle the provisioning of the necessary infrastructure for your app.

2. **Integrate with Databases**: Use managed database services like **AWS RDS, Azure SQL Database,** or **Google Cloud SQL** to store application data and allow for easy scaling without managing the database infrastructure yourself.

Step 3: Set Up SaaS Integrations

1. **Use SaaS for External Services**: Integrate with cloud-native SaaS services like **AWS S3** for file storage, **Google Cloud Vision** for image recognition, or **Azure Cognitive Services** for AI and machine learning functionalities. These services will extend the functionality of your application with minimal overhead.

2. **Deploy and Monitor the Application**: After deploying the application, use cloud-native monitoring tools like **AWS CloudWatch, Google Cloud Monitoring,** or **Azure Monitor** to ensure the application is running smoothly and efficiently.

Step 4: Testing and Optimization

1. **Test Performance**: Use load testing tools like **Apache JMeter** or **Artillery** to simulate traffic and test the performance of your application under various conditions. Adjust your infrastructure, scaling policies, and resource allocation as needed.

2. **Cost Optimization**: Review the cost of running your application on the cloud and identify areas for optimization, such as right-sizing instances or using reserved instances to reduce long-term costs.

Conclusion

With the foundation you've built throughout this book, you are now ready to embark on your cloud computing journey with confidence. Whether you're building applications, automating workflows, or exploring the cutting-edge technologies shaping the future of the cloud, the possibilities are endless. Keep learning, stay curious, and take on challenges as they come. Your cloud computing expertise will continue to grow, and the cloud world is waiting for you to shape it.

www.ingramcontent.com/pod-product-compliance
Lightning Source LLC
LaVergne TN
LVHW051333050326
832903LV00031B/3517